CAMBRIDGE
UNIVERSITY PRESS

ICT Starters

Next Steps Stage 1

Victoria Ellis, Sarah Lawrey and Doug Dickinson

CAMBRIDGE
UNIVERSITY PRESS

Shaftesbury Road, Cambridge CB2 8EA, United Kingdom

One Liberty Plaza, 20th Floor, New York, NY 10006, USA

477 Williamstown Road, Port Melbourne, VIC 3207, Australia

314–321, 3rd Floor, Plot 3, Splendor Forum, Jasola District Centre,
New Delhi – 110025, India

103 Penang Road, #05-06/07, Visioncrest Commercial, Singapore 238467

Cambridge University Press is part of the University of Cambridge.

It furthers the University's mission by disseminating knowledge in the pursuit of
education,learning and research at the highest international levels of excellence.

www.cambridge.org
Information on this title: www.cambridge.org/9781108463522

© Cambridge University Press & Assessment 2019

First published 2003
Second edition 2005
Third edition 2013
Fourth edition 2019

20 19 18 17 16 15 14

Printed in Malaysia by Vivar Printing

A catalogue record for this publication is available from the British Library

ISBN 978-1-108-46352-2 Paperback

Additional resources for this publication are available through Cambridge GO. Visit cambridge.org/go

Cambridge University Press has no responsibility for the persistence or accuracy
of URLs for external or third-party internet websites referred to in this publication,
and does not guarantee that any content on such websites is, or will remain,
accurate or appropriate. Information regarding prices, travel timetables, and other
factual information given in this work is correct at the time of first printing but
Cambridge University Press does not guarantee the accuracy of such information
thereafter.

All exam-style questions and sample answers in this title were written by the authors. In
examinations, the way marks are awarded may be different.

....

Cambridge ICT Starters: Next Steps 1 has been written to support you in your work for the Cambridge International Diploma ICT Starters syllabus (Next Steps Stage 1) from 2019. This book provides full coverage of all of the modules so that you will have a good platform of skills and information to support you in the next stages of your development of ICT capability. The modules can be studied in any order. The book supports your work on the key skills and basic routines needed at this level to become competent in handling data, basic spreadsheet management, creating and editing written work and handling images.

The book provides you and your helpers with:

- examples of activities to do
- exercises to practise the skills before you put them into practice
- final projects to show just how much you have learned
- optional scenario and challenge activities for those who want to challenge themselves further.

It is designed for use in the classroom with help and support from trained teachers. The tasks, skills and activities have been set in real situations where computer access will be essential. At the start of each module there is a section called 'Before you start' which explains what you need to know before you begin. The activities are designed to lead you towards a final project where you will have the opportunity to display your knowledge and understanding of each of the skills.

Some exercises require you to open prepared files for editing. These files are available to your teachers on **cambridge.org/go.** These files are included to help you start the activities in this book.

The modules in this book use Microsoft Office 2016, Microsoft Access and Microsoft Paint. Using these will develop your digital skills and will mean that the notes and activities in the book will be easy for you to follow. However, your teacher may decide to use different applications to help you to meet the module objectives.

We hope that you will enjoy working on this stage and will take pleasure in your learning.

Good luck!

Contents

Next Steps 1

Introduction

How to use this book

In every module, look out for these features:

Module objectives: This table shows you the key things that you will learn in this module.

	In this module, you will learn how to:	Pass/Merit	Done?
1	plan a short sequence of instructions (an algorithm)	P	
2	create a program as a sequence of instructions	P	

Key words: These boxes provide you with definitions of words that may be important or useful.

> **Key words**
>
> **Drop-down menu:** a box that has a list of different things for you to select.

Did you know?: These boxes provide interesting information and opportunities for further research.

> **Did you know?**
>
> An asterisk * in searches is called a wildcard.

Tip: These boxes give you handy hints as you work.

> **Tip**
>
> You can tell when you have selected an image as you will see a box appear around the edge of it.

Challenge: These activities are more difficult and extend beyond the syllabus.

> **Challenge**

Scenario: These are tasks that help you practise everything you have learned in the module in a "real-life" situation.

> **Scenario**
>
> **Far too busy!**

Pass/Merit: This shows you the level of all of the activities in the book.

> **Skill 6** P/M M P

Skill box: These boxes contain activities for you to test what you have learnt.

> **Skill 1**

Watch out!: These boxes help you to avoid making mistakes in your work.

> **!**
>
> **WATCH OUT!**
>
> Remember to save your document regularly.

	In this module, you will learn how to:	Pass/Merit	Done?
1	Create and edit a text document	P	
2	Edit text for a specific audience	P	
3	Add images or other objects to a document	P	
4	Refine and organise the layout of a document for a specific audience	M	
5	Evaluate a finished document (to make sure it does what it is meant to do).	M	

In this module, you are going to develop lots of exciting skills to help you work towards your final project. Many of these will help you learn how to edit and refine text in different ways, to suit different audiences.

Your final project will be to complete an article about healthy eating. You will need to carry out some research and select some suitable text and images. You will need to write about your findings for two groups of people: students at your school, and parents and carers.

You will also learn how to:

- add a border to a document
- add a border to an image
- rotate an image
- add SmartArt to a document.

Before you start

You should be able to:

- type words and sentences into a document using a keyboard
- use different keys on the keyboard such as letters, numbers, punctuation, shift, caps lock, backspace and enter
- select the words that you have typed so that you can make changes to them
- use a mouse to click on simple buttons, such as **Save**, **Print** and the **Spelling & Grammar checker**
- use a spellchecker to see if there are any spelling errors in your **text**
- choose a suitable name for the document that you have created
- proofread a document.

Introduction

The skills of typing and creating documents are very important. Having these skills means that you can produce a piece of work that is informative, clear, accurate and eye-catching.

One of the important things to think about when creating a document is your **audience**. In this module, you are going to learn how to create and change documents to make them suitable for different audiences.

Skill 1

Adding, changing and moving text

Adding text

When you open a document, you need to look for the flashing **cursor**. This will show you where text will appear when you start typing.

To type text into a document you use the keys on the keyboard. Each time you press a letter, number or symbol on the keyboard, it will appear in the document.

Changing text

If you decide that you want to change the text that you have typed, you can do this in three different ways:

1 You can use the backspace key [Backspace] to **delete** individual letters.

Did you know?

Most people can type 40 words in a minute, but a professional typist (someone who types as their job) can type 65 to 75 words in a minute. Now that's fast!

Key words

Text: the words that you type into a document.

Audience: the people who will read your document.

Cursor: a small vertical line in a document that flashes to show where text will appear when it is typed.

Key word

Delete: removing text or images from a document.

2 You can select a whole word by putting the mouse pointer on the word and **double-clicking** the left mouse button. When you press the backspace key, the whole word is deleted.

3 You can select a whole word or sentence by clicking and holding the left mouse button, then moving the cursor over the text you want to delete. You can tell the text is selected as it will have a different colour background like this:

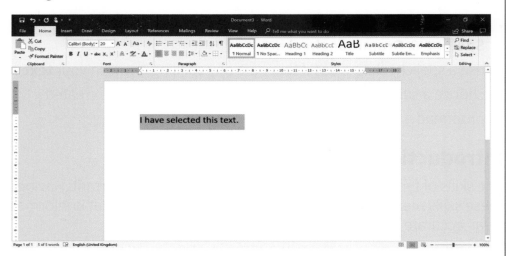

Moving text

When you have selected some text, you can also move it if it is in the wrong place.

You can move the text by placing the cursor in the middle of the selected text, clicking and holding down the left mouse button, and then dragging the cursor to where you want to put the text.

You can also move text by using the cut and paste options. If you select the text you want to move and click the right button on the mouse, you will see a menu where you can select the 'Cut' option in the **drop-down menu**. If you then move the cursor to the place where you want to put the text and click the right mouse button again, you can select the 'Paste' option in the drop-down menu to put the text into the new place in the document.

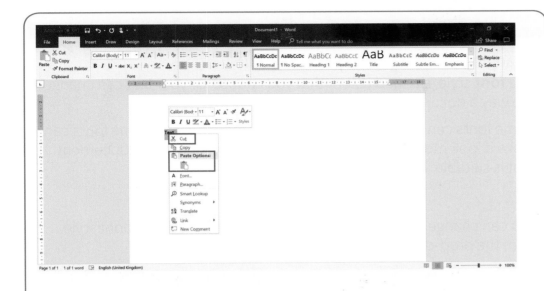

Activity 1.1

Open the document 'Holiday_Memories.docx' that your teacher will give you.

Add the following text to the end of the document:

> We also went to the beach. It was very warm and sunny. We played in the sea and built sandcastles.

Activity 1.2

The following sentence is in the wrong place:

> When we arrived, we had some tasty food at the restaurant in the hotel.

Move this sentence to the beginning of the document.

Activity 1.3

The following sentence is incorrect:

> The hotel was called The Beach Hotel.

Change the name of the hotel to 'The Sun and Sea Hotel'.

Activity 1.4

Save the document and print a copy of it.

Do you think 'Holiday_Memories' is a good filename for the document? Why?

Font: a particular style of typeface.

Changing the font style, size and colour

The **font** style, size and colour that you choose for your text can change the way a document looks.

Some fonts can make the document look more fun and some fonts can make it look more formal. You should choose a font for the document that is suitable for the audience.

Font style

You can change the style of the font by selecting a different font style from the drop-down menu.

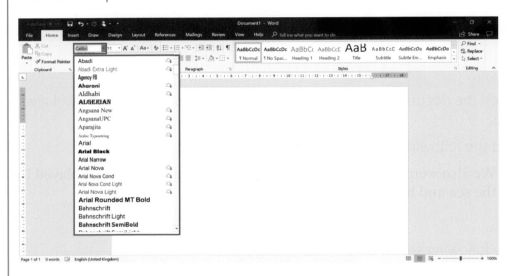

If you start typing, you should see that the text will look different.

Font size

You can select a different font size from the drop-down menu. The size of a font is called the point size and is often written as 10pt.

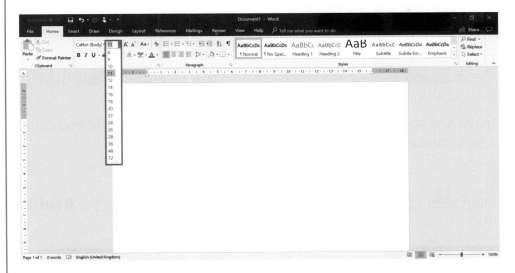

If you start typing, you should see the text becomes bigger or smaller.

Font colour

You can select a different font colour from the drop-down menu.

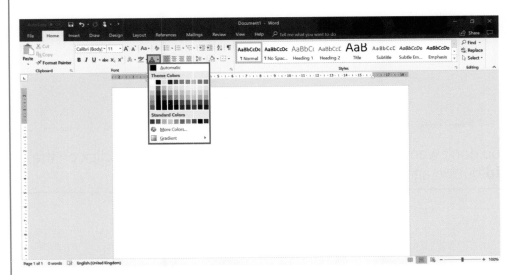

After you start typing, you should see that the text has changed colour.

Tip

You should avoid using more than two different fonts in a document as it can make it look messy and difficult to read.

Existing text

You can change the font style, size and colour of text that you have already typed by selecting the text and then choosing a font style, size or colour from the drop-down menu.

You may want to change the font style, size and colour of a title in a document to make it stand out from the other text.

Sometimes, you may want to make certain text more noticeable than other text around it.

To make text stand out, you could choose to change the font, or you could choose to make the text **bold**, <u>underlined</u> or in *italics*.

Bold

You can select the text you want to make bold, then click on the **Bold** button.

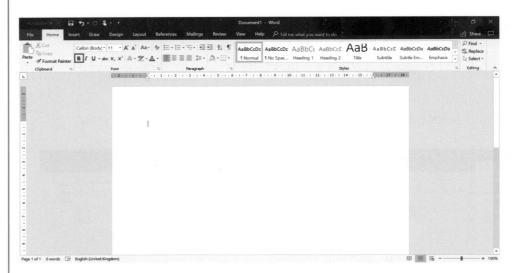

If you don't want the text to be bold any more, you can just click on the **Bold** button again and it will remove the bold from the text.

Underline and italics

To make the text underlined or italics, you just click on the **Italics** button or the **Underline** button.

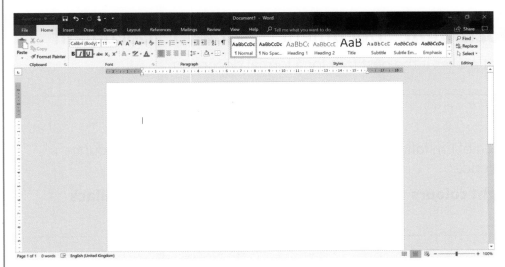

Activity 2.1

Look at the file 'Info_about_vegetables.docx' that your teacher will give you.

What text in the file would you make **bold?**

_____

What text in the file would you <u>underline</u>?

_____

What text in the file would you make *italics*?

_____

Activity 2.2

Which of the following fonts would be the best for someone the same age as you?

Menu   Menu   *Menu*   Menu

What makes it the best font for someone the same age as you?

_____

Activity 2.3

Which of the following fonts would be the best for a formal document?

Document   Document   _Document_   **Document**

What makes it the best font for a formal document?

_____

Activity 2.4

Which of the following font colours would be the best for a young audience?

Bright colours   **Pale colours**   **Black**

_____

What makes those the best colours for a young audience?

_____

Activity 2.5

Open the document 'Menu.docx' that your teacher will give you.

Edit the font style in the document to make it suitable for an audience of 8- to 13-year olds.

Edit the title and subtitles in the document to make them stand out more. The subtitles are the names of each of the menu items.

Explain to your friend or your teacher how the changes that you have made make the document suitable for an audience of 8- to 13-year olds.

Activity 2.6

Open the document 'Memo.docx' that your teacher will give you.

Change the font in the document to make it suitable for an adult audience.

Edit the title in the document to make it bigger so it stands out more.

Explain to your friend or your teacher how the changes that you have made make the document suitable for an audience of adults.

Skill 3

Changing the alignment of text

The alignment of text means where the text is placed on the page. There are three main alignments that you need to know about for this module.

They are:

- left align
- centre align
- right align

The text that you have been typing so far will be left aligned. Left align means that all the text that you type will be lined up down the left side of the page.

The opposite of this is right align. This is when all the text that you type will line up down the right side of the page. Centre align is when the text that you type is placed in the centre of the page, at equal distances from the right side and the left side of the page.

To change the alignment of text you need to select the text first. When you have selected the text you can click on the **Alignment** buttons. The **Alignment** buttons can be found on the **Home** tab in the **Paragraph** section. They look like lots of horizontal lines. The first button is left align, the second is centre align and the third is right align.

> **Tip**
>
> Left align is the default setting that the software has.

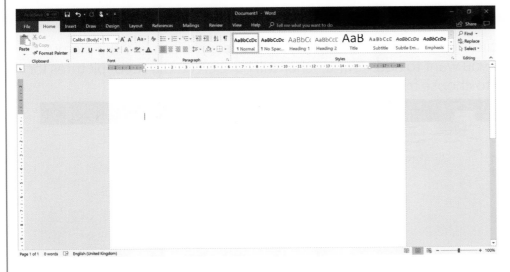

Activity 3.1

Open the document 'Menu.docx'.

Type your name at the bottom of the document and make it right aligned.

Key words

Image: a picture, photo or diagram.

Insert: to add something in a specific place.

Skill 4

Adding images and borders into a document

You may want to add an **image** into your document.

Adding images

You can add an image into a document by moving the cursor to the line that you want to add the image and clicking on the **Insert** tab.

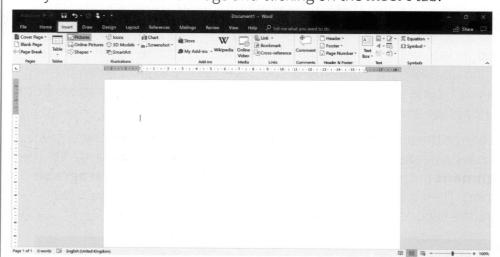

By clicking on the button that says **Pictures**, you can find the picture that you want to add. Your teacher will have created a set of pictures for you to choose from.

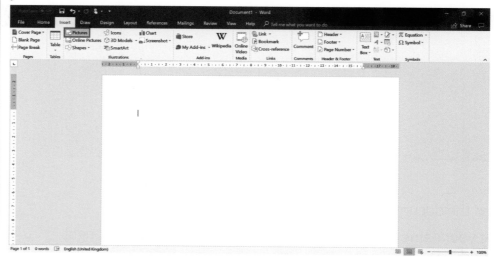

If you click on 'Insert', you will now see the picture in your document.

Adding borders

You can add a border to a document by clicking on the **Design** tab.

You can now choose a border for the page by clicking on the **Page Borders** button.

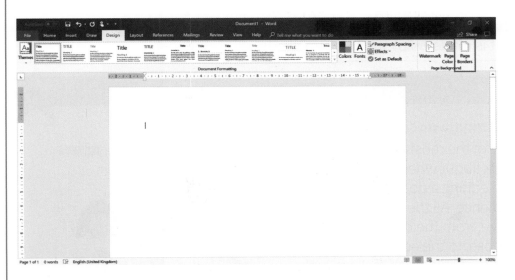

Here you can choose a border for the page and a style, colour and width for that border.

Activity 4.1

Open the document 'Menu.docx' that your teacher will give you.

Insert the image 'Vegetables.jpg' between the lines '**We also have the best selection of vegetables**' and '**We hope you enjoy your food**'.

Activity 4.2

Add a border to the document 'Menu.docx'.

Choose a box border, in a style that is a dotted line, like this:

…………………..

Make the border a width of 1pt and coloured blue.

Activity 4.3

Change the border in the document 'Menu.docx'. Choose an art border that is made up of stars.

Key word

Refine: to improve or change.

Skill 5

M

Refining a document for an audience

One of the most important things to think about when you are creating and editing a document is your audience. All the decisions that you make, from the content that you choose, to the editing decisions you make, should be to make sure that the document is suitable for your audience.

You and your teacher may have different ideas about what a document should look like. You may want a document to be more colourful and fun to get people's attention. An adult may find a document in this style too childish and may not want to read it.

The actual content of the document may need to be looked at as well. You may want the text to be informal. An adult may want the text to be more formal in order for people to take it seriously, especially if it is a serious matter.

The images should also match the feel of the text. For example, a document would look odd if the text was formal, but the images were cartoons. So, you need to think carefully about the images you choose and whether they match the text.

The layout can also be important. If you want an informal feel, you may make the images quite large in the document and place them in a fun way. If you want to make a document have a more formal feel, you may choose fewer images and make them smaller.

Making a document look formal doesn't mean it needs to look boring. It just needs to look simple and have a readable font and style.

The question you should ask yourself each time you make a decision about content or editing is 'what would my audience want?'

Activity 5.1

Open the document 'Healthy_Eating_Letter.docx' that your teacher will give you.

The content and style of this document is very muddled. It is meant to be a formal letter from a school to parents and carers telling them about an information evening they can attend.

Look carefully at the document and think carefully about the audience.

Discuss with a friend what is unsuitable about the document for the audience.

Edit the document to make it more suitable for the audience.

Activity 5.2

Write a paragraph of text about the changes that you made to the document. Explain why the document is now more suitable for the audience.

> **Tip**
>
> An unprofessional document might look too busy or messy. This is often because too many different font styles, sizes and colours have been used.

Far too busy!

A quick guide to healthy eating has been created to hand out at school. You look at the document and realise that the style is muddled, messy and crowded (there is too much on the page).

Your task is to use your new skills to edit the document. It needs to be fun and appealing to students at the school, but it also needs to look formal.

Activity 1

Open the document 'Heathy_Eating_Guide.docx'.

Discuss with a friend what mistakes have been made when creating and editing the document.

Activity 2

Edit the document to make it suitable for the audience, making sure that it looks formal.

Activity 3

Show your edited document to another friend. Explain what you have changed about the document and how you have made it suitable for the audience.

Challenge

Editing images

You have learnt how to insert an image into a document. You will now learn how to edit that image in a couple of ways to make it look a little different.

Adding a border

To make an image stand out more, you can add a border to it.

To add a border to an image, you first need to select the image by moving the mouse pointer over it and clicking the left mouse button.

Tip

You can tell when you have selected an image as you will see a box appear around the edge of it.

When you have selected the image, you will see a **Format** tab appear. If you click on the **Format** tab you can find the **Picture Border** button. Clicking on the **Picture Border** button makes a drop-down box appear.

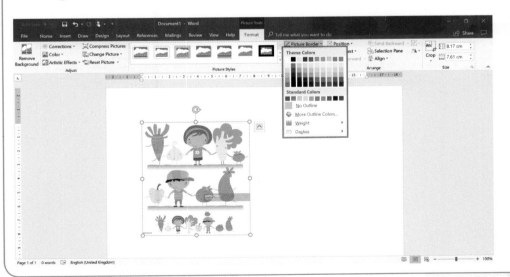

Key word

Format: the way something is arranged or presented.

You can:

- select a colour for your border by clicking on one of the colours in the drop-down menu
- select a weight for your border (the weight of the border means how thick the border will be)
- add a border to your image by using the preset border options that appear in the area to the left of the **Picture Border** button.

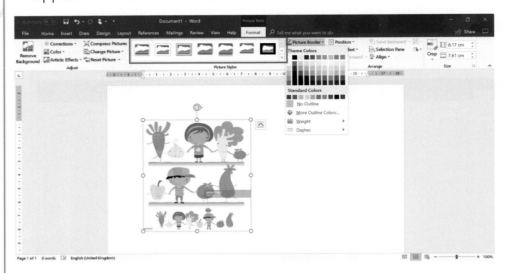

Rotating an image

To make an image look a little different, or to fit an image into a certain space, you may need to rotate it. When you rotate an image, you turn it in a circular path.

To rotate an image, you will need to select the image first.

When you have selected the image, you will see a box appear around it. At the top of the box you should see a circular arrow.

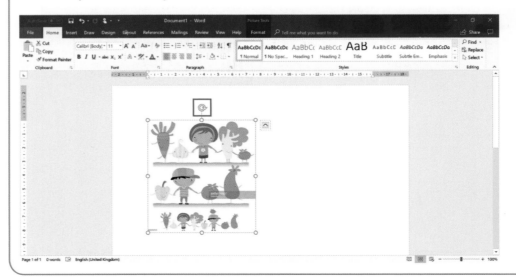

When you move your mouse pointer over the circular arrow and click and hold down the left mouse button, you will see the image start to rotate when you move your mouse. When the image is at the angle that you want it, stop clicking the left mouse button.

SmartArt

If you have a diagram to add to a document, one way that you can do this is using SmartArt. SmartArt is a graphic building tool that helps you create simple graphics or diagrams to present information clearly.

You can add SmartArt by moving the cursor to the place you want in the document.

You can click on the **Insert** tab and then click on the **SmartArt** button.

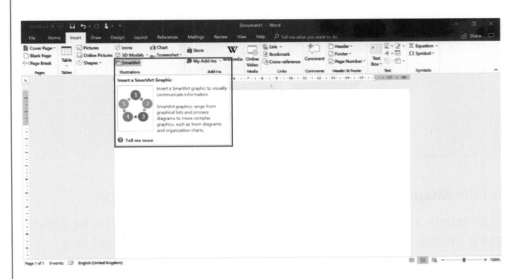

When you have chosen a SmartArt, click on the image of it and then click on 'OK'. This will then put the SmartArt into your document.

It will have places for you to type in the text you want, like this:

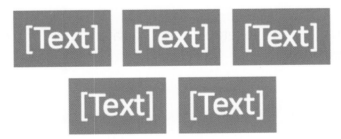

If you want to add text to the boxes, you need to move the cursor to a place that says '[Text]' and click the left mouse button. You can then type text into the box.

You can change the colour of the boxes in the SmartArt.

You can select a box to change the colour by moving the cursor to the box and clicking the left mouse button. You can then select the **Format** tab that appears.

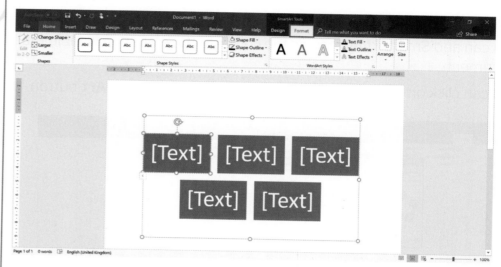

Select the **Shape Fill** button and select a colour for the shape.

You can delete any of the boxes in the SmartArt by selecting the box and pressing the backspace key. This will delete the box and the text in it.

Activity 1
Open the document 'Menu.docx'.

Add a thick dark-blue border to the image of the vegetables.

Activity 2
Rotate the image of the vegetables until it is at an angle. You could rotate to a 45-degree angle.

Activity 3
Open the document 'Memo.docx'.

Insert the SmartArt called Basic Block List at the bottom of the document. Delete two of the boxes.

Insert one of the following words into each box that is left:

Parents

Teachers

Students

Activity 4
Change the colour of the boxes in the SmartArt to make them red, green and blue.

Final project – Healthy body, healthy mind!

Your teacher wants to make sure that all the students in the school, and their parents and carers, are eating healthily. They want you to write an **article** describing what healthy eating means.

> **Key word**
>
> **Article:** a piece of writing in a magazine or a newspaper.

You are going to need to consider two different audiences:

- the students at your school
- the parents and carers of students at the school.

You will need to adapt the article to suit each of the given audiences and give your teacher both versions.

You will work with other students to research the content you want to include. It is then your job as the editor to take the information and edit it to make it suitable for each audience. This is a chance to show how excellent your word-processing skills have become!

Activity 1

Find a partner to work with to research some suitable information for your healthy eating article. Choose content (text and images) that is suitable for the parent and carers audience first.

Share the research that you find with another pair in your class. Save all the content that you have gathered into a document.

Activity 2

On your own, look at the content that you have gathered and edit it to create an article to give to parents and carers.

Choose the text and the images carefully to make the article suitable for your audience. Make sure the document looks appealing, but also formal.

Activity 3

On your own, look at the content that you gathered and edit it to create an article to give to other students. Make sure the document looks fun to read, but that it doesn't look too messy or crowded.

Choose the text and the images carefully. Make sure that the language used is appropriate for the audience and make sure the images are attractive and eye-catching.

Activity 4

Swap both of your articles with a partner. You should now have two articles from a different student in your class. **Proofread** the articles that you have been given and tell the student who wrote them about any errors that you find.

Key word

Proofread: when you read through all the text in a document to see if you can find any mistakes.

Reflection

1 What can you do to a document to make it look more formal?

_____

_____

_____

2 What choices did you make for your article, to make sure it would be good for the students in your school?

_____

_____

_____

_____

3 Why did the things you changed for the article for the school magazine make it better for an older audience?

_____

_____

_____

_____

	In this module, you will learn how to:	Pass/Merit	Done?
1	Create repeating patterns, using stamps and/or copy tools	P	
2	Create pictures, using different tools and effects	P	
3	Select appropriate objects, copy and resize them	M	
4	Save drafts showing the development of the design.	M	

In this module, you are going to develop skills to help you work towards your final project, which will be to create an exciting image that tells everyone about your favourite book.

Books can be fun, entertaining, fascinating and very informative. You will be able to show your creativity in your book image by including some new skills that you will learn. These skills will help you to edit the image by rotating it, flipping it and resizing it.

Using brush tools will also show that you can create pictures using lots of different tools and effects. You will also learn about version control when you create images and why it is used.

You will also learn how to:

- crop an image
- add text to an image.

Before you start

You should be able to:

- use a mouse, including clicking the left and right buttons
- save an image with a suitable filename
- draw a line
- draw a simple shape, such as a square or a circle
- use different brush tools
- fill the shape with a colour
- select all or part of an image
- copy and paste an image.

Introduction

Using computers to create and **edit** art and images is an interesting and creative skill.

Computers have been used to create **digital art** and images for over 50 years.

Modern digital art can be very detailed and it takes a lot of skill to create the images. Look at the amazing digital image on the next page. Although you will be creating something much simpler in this module, you might eventually be able to create an image like this when you are older. Everyone has to start somewhere!

In this module, you will be using software called Microsoft Paint to create and edit your images. Microsoft Paint is simple software to use and it has lots of different tools that allow you to be very creative and imaginative with images. (Your teacher will show you where to find it on your computer at school and how to open a new file.)

Key words

Edit: to change the look of an image.

Digital art: an image that has been created using a computer.

Did you know?

Microsoft Paint is used by some professional artists to create images. You can find some of these online if you search for 'images created using Microsoft Paint'.

So, you are now going to have fun creating your own images using new flip, rotate and resize skills.

To do this, you need to know how to select the images first by using the **Select** tool. You can select the image, or part of the image, by using the rectangular selection and drawing a box around it. You can also select the image, or part of the image, by using the free-form selection tool and drawing a line around it.

WATCH OUT!

You should never copy the work of another person and say that it is your own. If you use an image created by someone else in your work, you should always ask their permission. If you copy it without their permission and say that it is your own, this is called **plagiarism**.

Skill 1

Importing an image

When you create an image, you may need to **import** other image files into it. You can import image files from many different places. You may want to import them from your mobile phone or a digital camera.

You could also import them from the internet, from a file that you have scanned into a computer or from a clipart collection of images.

You are going to import files from a saved images source.

To import an image file, you need to:

- click on the **File** tab
- click on 'Open'
- find the image file that you want to import and click on 'Open'.

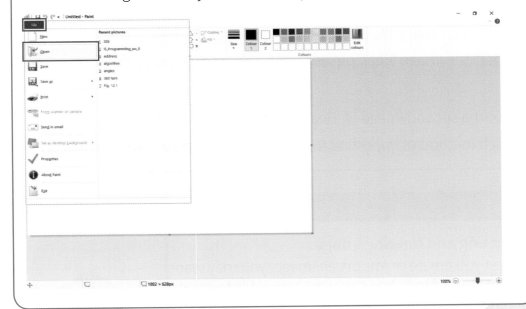

Key word

Import: to bring a different file into the program that you are using.

WATCH OUT!

Remember to keep yourself safe if you search for images online. Only choose search results that look like they are from an age-appropriate and reliable source.

WATCH OUT!

Your teacher will discuss with you the importance of getting the agreement of the person who owns the image, before using it. Your teacher should also discuss the importance of getting permission from another person if you want to take an image of them and share it.

You can also import an image by clicking on the **Paste** button and clicking on 'Paste from'.

Activity 1.1

Open the Microsoft Paint software and create a new file. Your teacher will give you an image file called 'Bear.jpg'.

Import the image 'Bear.jpg' using the 'File' and 'Open' options.

Activity 1.2

Import a second image of 'Bear.jpg' using the 'Paste from' option.

Which method of importing the image did you find worked best for you?

Key words

Rotate: to move an image around in a circular path.

Flip: to turn an image over.

Skill 2

Rotating and flipping images

When you create or import an image, you may want to **rotate** or **flip** it. You can use these skills to create interesting, symmetrical patterns.

When you rotate an image, you turn it around in a circular path. When you flip an image, it is like turning it over to create a mirror image.

To rotate an image, you first need to make sure that you have selected the image. When you have selected the image you can click on the **Rotate** button.

You will now be able to see that you can rotate the image left or right by 90 degrees.

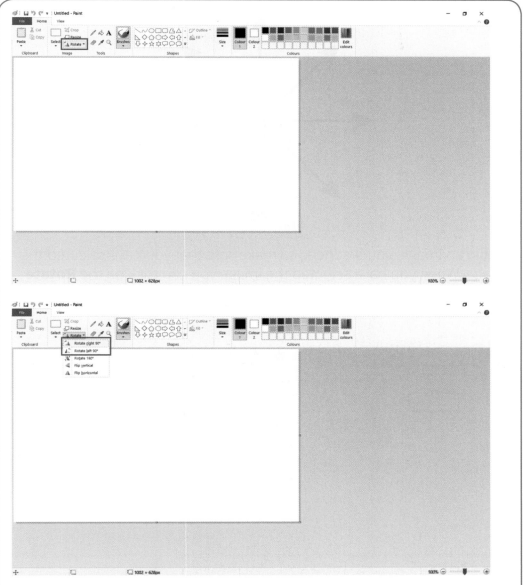

If you rotate the image to the right by 90 degrees, it will turn the image to the right by one quarter of a circle. If you rotate the image to the left by 90 degrees, it will turn the image to the left by one quarter of a circle.

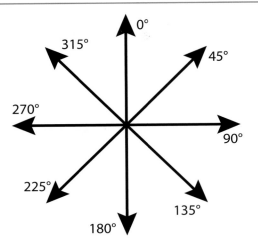

To flip an image, you first need to make sure that you have selected the image. When you have selected the image you can click on the **Rotate** button. You will now be able to see that you can flip the image vertically or horizontally.

A vertical line is one that is drawn from the top to the bottom on a page. When you flip an image vertically, it is like turning the image over so that the bottom of the image is now the top.

Imagine if you had a poster and you turned it over by taking the bottom and putting it where the top was. This would be like flipping an image vertically.

Vertical flip 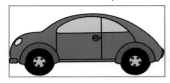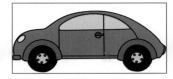 Horizontal flip

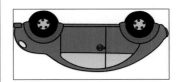

A horizontal line is one that is drawn from side to side on a page. When you flip an image horizontally, it is like turning over the image so that the left side has become the right side.

Activity 2.1

Open a new Microsoft Paint file. Draw an arrow pointing to the right with the Arrow Shape tool.

Draw a second arrow pointing to the right with the Arrow Shape tool.

Rotate this arrow 90 degrees to the right.

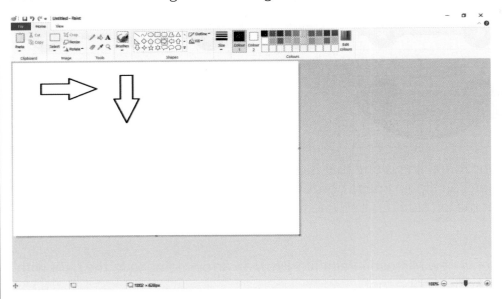

Draw a third arrow pointing to the right.

Rotate this arrow until it is pointing to the left.

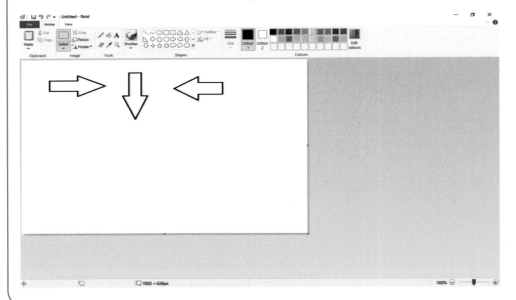

Activity 2.2

Open a new Microsoft Paint file. Import the image 'Flower.png'.

Make a copy of the 'Flower.png' image at the side of the first one.

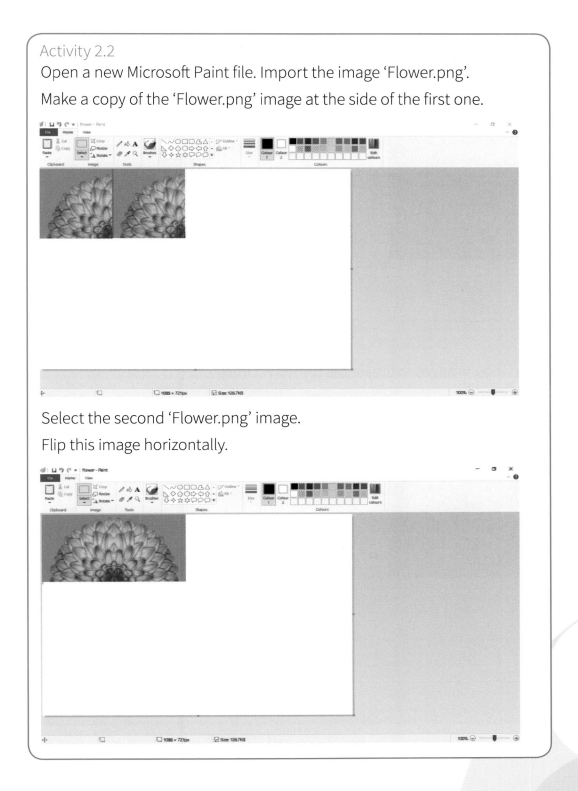

Select the second 'Flower.png' image.

Flip this image horizontally.

Make two more copies of the 'Flower.png' image, below the first two.

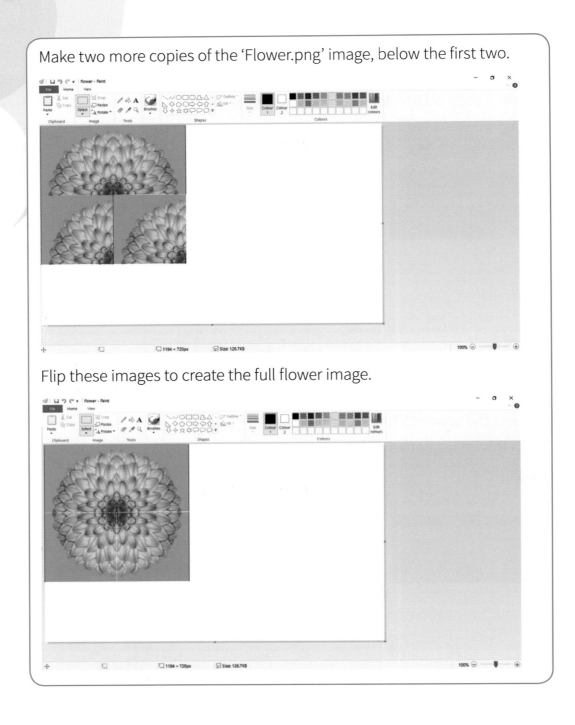

Flip these images to create the full flower image.

Activity 2.3

Open a new Microsoft Paint file. Using at least two different brush tools, draw half a butterfly. For example:

When you have drawn half of your butterfly, select what you have drawn, copy it and flip it to make a whole butterfly image.

Save your butterfly image with a suitable filename.

Activity 2.4

Open a new Microsoft Paint file. Using at least two different brush tools, draw a garden background.

Import at least two of your butterfly images.

Rotate your butterfly images to make them appear to be flying around your garden.

Save your garden image with a suitable filename.

Skill 3

Resizing an image

When you create or import an image, you may want to make it bigger or smaller.

You can do this by **resizing** it.

There are two ways that you can resize an image.

Using the Resize tool

You can select the image that you want to resize by clicking on the **Select** button and drawing a box around the part of the image you want to resize.

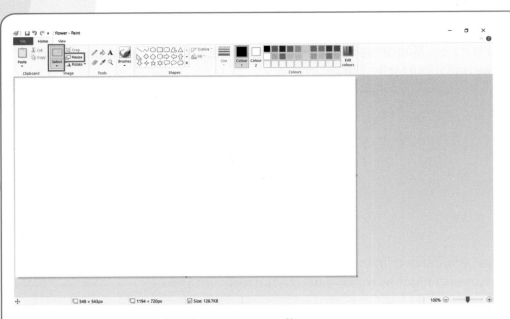

If you click on the **Resize** button you will see a menu.

If you make sure that the box that says 'Maintain aspect ratio' is ticked, this will make sure that the image doesn't **distort** when you resize it.

You can change the size for 'Horizontal' from 100% to a bigger or smaller number. The 'Vertical' size will change automatically.

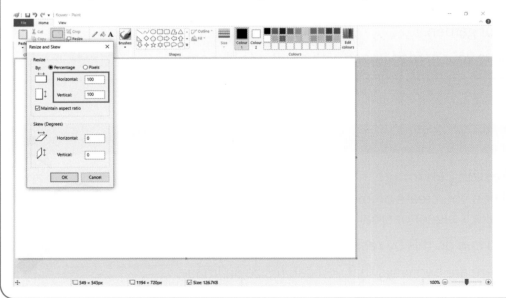

40

The image will appear bigger if you make the number bigger, for example 150%.

It will appear smaller if you make the number smaller, for example 50%.

Using the resize arrows

To resize an image using the resize arrows, first select the part of the image that you want to resize.

Then move the cursor to a corner of the image and you should see the cursor change to an arrow that looks like this ←→. When you see the arrow, click and hold the left mouse button.

You can then move the cursor to make the image bigger or smaller. You move the cursor toward the image to make it smaller and away from the image to make it bigger.

Activity 3.1

Import the image 'Bear.jpg' that your teacher will give you. Use the resize tool to change the size of the image to 85 per cent.

Activity 3.2

Import a second 'Bear.jpg' image. Use the arrow tool to make the image small.

Activity 3.3

Import three other 'Bear.jpg' images.

Make each bear a different size using the resize tool or arrow tool. Line the bears up from largest to smallest.

Skill 4

Version control

When you are creating images, you may need to create different versions of the image until you have a final version that you are happy with. These different versions are called **drafts**. You should save each of these draft versions so that you can see the progress of your image.

Key word

Draft: a first attempt or early attempt at creating something.

If you save each draft version, then if you don't like something, it is easy to go back to an earlier draft of it and try again.

You should give each of these draft versions a suitable filename. The filename should show which draft version number that is. For example, if you are creating an image that shows a garden you may have the following names for the draft versions:

'My_Garden_v1.png'

'My_Garden_v2.png'

'My_Garden_v3.png'

'My_Garden_Final.png'

The first three files are draft versions and the last file is the final version. Naming the files in this way is called version control. It allows you to see the order in which the draft versions were created.

Activity 4.1

Can you think of two reasons why it is good to have draft versions of your image?

Activity 4.2

Can you think why version control is important?

Scenario

Time for fun in the sun!

You are going to create your very own beach picture. Think about what you like to do on the beach. What will you include in your picture?

Activity 1

Create the background for your beach picture.

Use the brush tools to create the sand, sea and sky.

Save this image as 'Beach_v1.png'.

Activity 2

Your teacher will give you some images to use. Import the image 'Beachball.jpg' into your beach picture. Resize the beach ball so that it fits appropriately on your beach. You don't want an enormous beach ball taking up most of the picture! Save this image as 'Beach_v2.png'.

Activity 3

Import the image 'BeachUmbrella.jpg' into your beach picture. Import a second image of 'BeachUmbrella.jpg' into your beach picture.

Select each umbrella and place them at either side of your picture.

Draw a sandcastle with the brush tools between the umbrellas.

Save this image as 'Beach_v3.png'.

Activity 4

Open the version of your image 'Beach_v2.png'. Add a boat to the sea.

Save this image as 'Beach_v4.png'.

Activity 5

Decide whether you like your image 'Beach_v3.png' or 'Beach_v4.png' better and open this file. Finish your beach picture using the brush tools, adding any other things that you want to the picture.

Save this image as 'Beach_Final.png'.

Adding text to an image

To add text to an image you click on the **Text** button.

Move your mouse pointer to the point on the page that you want to add the text and click the left mouse button.

You will see a box appear that has a dotted line around it.

You can now type and you will see the text appear in this box.

Activity 1

Import the image 'Bear.jpg'. Add the following text below the image:

'Some bears sleep for the whole winter!'

Cropping an image

When you import an image, you may find that you only want part of the image and not all of it. You can remove part of an image by **cropping** it.

Select the part of the image that you want to keep by using the Select tool.

When you have selected the part that you want to keep you can click on the **Crop** button.

This will remove all the parts of the image that you did not select and just leave the part that you did select.

Activity 2

Import the image 'Bear.jpg'. Crop the trees out of the image so that you are just left with the bear.

Tip

You need to select the part that you want to keep, not the part that you want to remove.

Final project – What's your favourite book?

You are going to create an image that could be used as a poster to advertise your favourite book. Try to use all the skills that you have learnt, including importing files, different brush tools, copy and paste, flip, rotate and version control. This is your chance to show the skills you have learnt!

Activity 1

Create a first draft of your image.

Ask two of your friends for feedback about your image.

Ask them to comment on two things that they think are good about your poster and one thing that they think you could improve.

Activity 2

Create a second draft of your image.

Ask the same friends if they think the first draft or the second draft is better.

Save the draft that you and your friends like better as your final draft.

Reflection

1 Which is your favourite brush tool to use? Why do you like this one the best?

_____

_____

_____

2 Why should you create draft versions of your work?

_____

_____

_____

3 Why should you never copy the work of other people and say it is your own work?

_____

_____

_____

	In this module, you will learn how to:	Pass/Merit	Done?
1	Enter labels and numbers into a spreadsheet	P	
2	Enter and copy simple formulas	P	
3	Create a graph	P	
4	Change data	M	
5	Use a spreadsheet to answer a modelled scenario ('what if').	M	

In this module, you are going to develop skills to help you work towards your final project. This project will be about going on a school trip to the Techno Computer Museum. There is a lot to organise when going on a school trip! You are going to help your teachers plan all the details using a spreadsheet.

You will also learn how to:

- create a spreadsheet to calculate the costs of taking students on a school trip
- enter formulas and use functions in the spreadsheet to work out how much each student will need to pay for the trip
- create graphs and answer 'what if' questions, such as 'What will happen if the cost of the coach increases?'
- use the functions AVERAGE, MIN and MAX
- format the spreadsheet to make the layout better.

Before you start

You should:

- have used formulas in maths to do calculations
- know how to use graphs
- know how to create graphs to show different types of information
- have used software to make tables and graphs from data you have been given
- know how to enter data and text into a computer
- know how to use copy and paste
- have saved work before, and opened saved work.

Introduction

A **spreadsheet** is a piece of software made up of a grid that allows you to enter text and numbers, and lets you make **calculations** using **formulas**. You can also use it to make graphs and charts.

Spreadsheets are used by people and companies all around the world to store data and make calculations, such as working out how much money they have made and how much money they have spent.

Your teacher might use spreadsheets to work out how much a school trip will cost (coach hire, entrance fee, lunch), so they know how much each student needs to pay.

Key words

Spreadsheet: a piece of software that has a grid made up of rows and columns. It is used to help people do calculations.

Calculate: to mathematically work out the result. A calculation is the way the result is worked out.

Formula: a mathematical calculation in spreadsheets that uses symbols (+, -, *, /) to calculate results.

Microsoft Excel is the spreadsheet software that will be used in this module, but there are lots of others you could use, such as Numbers and Google Sheets.

Skill 1

What is a spreadsheet?

A spreadsheet is made up of **cells**, which are the individual boxes in the spreadsheet. The letters across the top represent the **columns**, the numbers down the side represent the **rows**.

Each cell has a **reference** that is made up of the column (the letter) and the row (the number) that the cell is in.

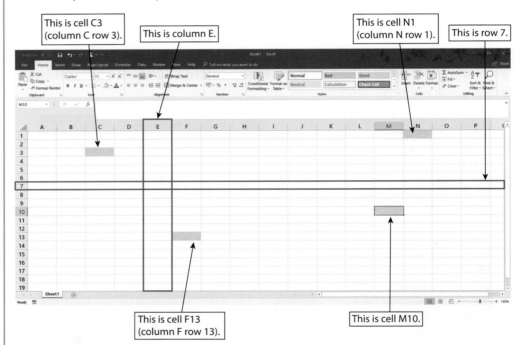

This is cell C3 (column C row 3).

This is column E.

This is cell N1 (column N row 1).

This is row 7.

This is cell F13 (column F row 13).

This is cell M10.

Activity 1.1

You are going to play a game called 'Find those cells!' with a partner. One of you will be Player 1, the other will be Player 2. Both players should draw a grid with 8 columns and 8 rows on separate pieces of paper. Label each column with a letter A–H. Label each row with a number 1–8.

Without your partner seeing your grid, colour in:

	A	B	C	D	E	F	G	H
1								
2								
3								
4								
5								
6								
7								
8								

- one row of five cells
- one row of four cells
- one column of three cells
- one column of two cells.

This is an example grid.

The aim of the game is to find all the cells your partner coloured in on their grid. Each group of cells represents a ship.

1. Player 1 gives a cell reference (letter, then number) to Player 2.
2. Player 2 tells Player 1 if they have coloured in that cell or not. Player 1 puts an X if there is no ship, and colours it in if there is a ship.
3. Player 2 gives a cell reference to Player 1.
4. Player 1 tells Player 2 if they have coloured in that cell or not.
5. Take it in turns to ask questions and repeat until one player has found all fourteen cells. That player has won the game.

Activity 1.2

You are now going to practise identifying cells. Open the spreadsheet 'identifyingCells.xlsx' that your teacher will give you.

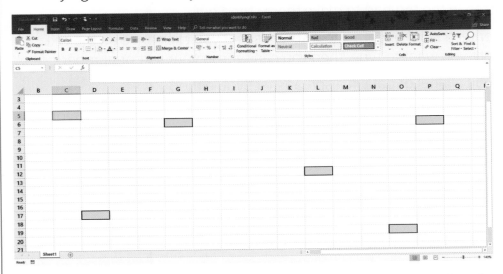

There are ten cells highlighted in yellow. Type the cell reference of each cell inside it (remember the cell reference is the column then the number).

Check with a partner that you agree with their cell references.

Entering data into a spreadsheet

You can enter text and numbers into a spreadsheet.

A label is a piece of text that describes what is being entered; for example it might be a heading or a title.

Data can be text or **numeric** and is entered into the spreadsheet. It might then be used to do calculations.

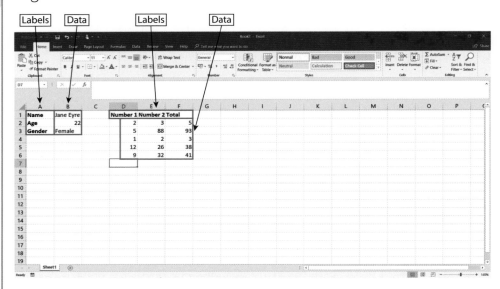

The labels in this image have been formatted as bold (using the **Bold** button in the toolbar) to make them stand out.

To enter a label or data into a spreadsheet you click once on the cell where you want to type, then you can type in your text or numbers.

To edit a label or data in a spreadsheet you either:

- double-click on the cell you want to change then edit the text, or
- click once on the cell and change the text in the formula bar at the top.

Click in the formula bar to change the text.

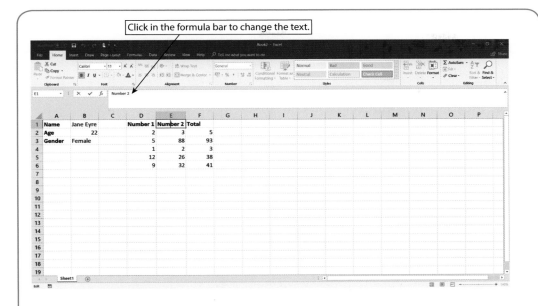

Activity 2.1

Open the spreadsheet 'firstformula.xlsx' that has the labels 'First Number' and 'Second Number' already entered.

First Number	Second Number
12	6
5	25
44	33

Enter the numbers from the table into the spreadsheet under the appropriate labels.

WATCH OUT!

Remember to save your document regularly.

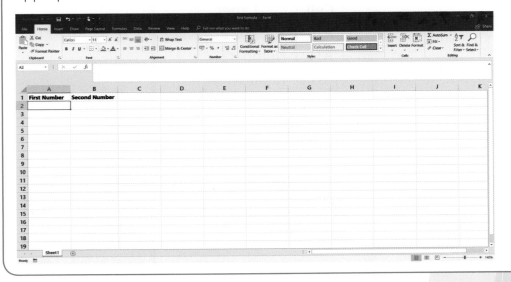

Activity 2.2
Add the label '**Total**' into the cell C1 in the spreadsheet 'firstformula.xlsx'.

Activity 2.3
Enter the following labels in the cells given in the table:

Cell	Label
F1	1
G1	2
H1	3
I1	4
J1	5
E2	1
E3	2
E4	3
E5	4
E6	5

Activity 2.4
Change the label in cell A1 to 'Number1', and the label in cell B1 to 'Number2'.

Activity 2.5
Enter the following labels in the cells given in the table:

Cell	Label
A10	Number1
A11	Number2
A12	Addition
A13	Subtraction
A14	Division
A15	Multiplication

Your spreadsheet should now look like this image. If your columns are not wide enough (and the text is cut off) you can make them wider by holding down the left mouse button and moving the line between the column headers (inside the red box on the image).

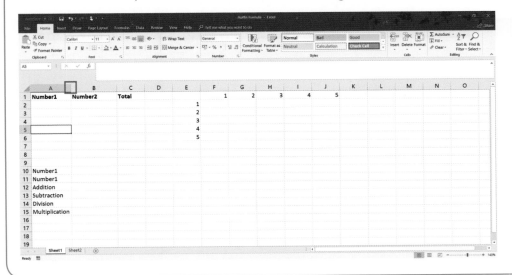

Tip

Save your document by giving it a useful name, with your initials at the end. You will need it for a later Skill.

Skill 3

Using simple formulas with numbers

In mathematics you use symbols for addition, subtraction, division and multiplication.

In a spreadsheet you use these symbols:

Calculation	Symbol	Examples
Addition	+	$1+2=3$
		$2+2=4$
		$10+12=22$
Subtraction	–	$2-1=1$
		$10-5=5$
		$11-4=7$
Division	/	$10/2=5$
		$20/10=2$
		$15/3=5$
Multiplication	*	$2*2=4$
		$5*2=10$
		$10*3=30$

In a spreadsheet you can enter a formula into a cell. The formula <u>must</u> start with an equals sign (=).

In the cell A1, the formula =1+2 is typed. When you click on Enter on the keyboard, the result will appear in the same cell.

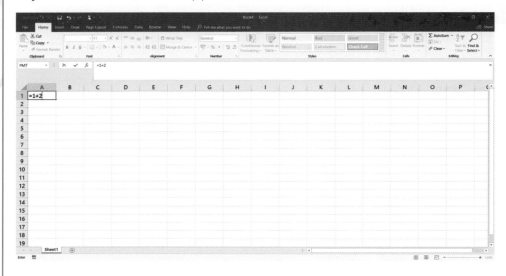

The result.

You can still see the formula in the formula bar.

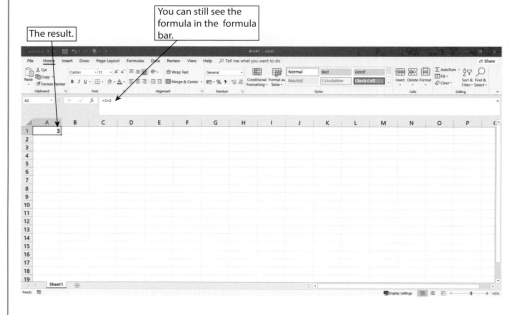

Activity 3.1

Create a new spreadsheet.

Open Microsoft Excel to create a new file.

Click on **File** and then **Save As**.

Give your spreadsheet a meaningful name and save it in a suitable folder.

Type the formulas (shown in the table below) into the given cells.

Cell	Formula
A1	=2+5
B1	=5-2
C1	=10/2
D1	=10*2

Tip

Remember to put **=** at the start.

Activity 3.2
In cell A2 write a formula to add the numbers 2 and 3 together.

Activity 3.3
In cell B2 write a formula to subtract 4 from 10.

Tip

Subtracting 2 from 5 would be 5-2.

Activity 3.4
In cell C2 write a formula to divide 12 by 4.

Tip

Dividing 20 by 2 would be 20/2.

Activity 3.5
In cell D2 write a formula to multiply 3 by 8.

Skill 4

Using simple formulas with cells

In a spreadsheet you do not need to type the numbers you want to use in a formula. You can use the cell reference (for example, A1).

In the image, the numbers in cells A1 and B1 need to be added together.

In cell C1, instead of writing =2+5, you can write =A1+B1.

Tip

Instead of writing A1 and B1, you can just click on them.

Type the =.

Click on the cell A1 with your left mouse button.

Type the +.

Click on the cell B1 with your left mouse button.

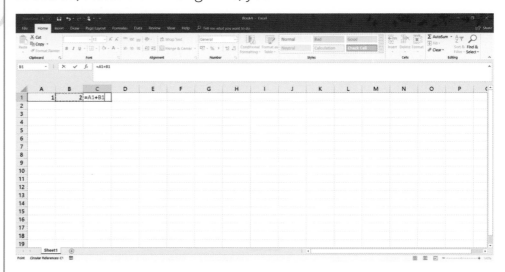

For these tasks you will need to open your completed spreadsheet from **Skill 2**, 'firstformula.xlsx'.

Activity 4.1

Enter a number in cell A2 and another number in cell B2.

In cell C2 enter the formula =A2+B2.

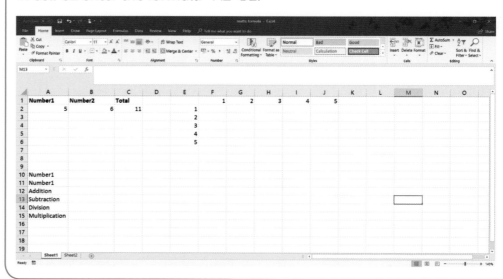

Activity 4.2

Enter any number in cell B10 and another number in cell B11.

In cell B12 enter a formula to add B10 and B11.

Activity 4.3

In cell B13 enter a formula to calculate B10–B11.

Activity 4.4

In cell B14 enter a formula to calculate B10/B11.

Activity 4.5

In cell B15 enter a formula to calculate B10*B11.

Activity 4.6

Enter any number in cell A3 and another number in B3.

In cell C3 enter a formula to add together the numbers in A2, B2, A3 and B3.

Activity 4.7

The cells E1 to J6 can create a multiplication grid.

In cell F2 write a formula to multiply F1 by E2.

In cell F3 write a formula to multiply F1 by E3.

In cell F3 write a formula to multiply F1 by E4.

Continue for cells F5 and F6.

In cell G2 write a formula to multiply G1 by E2. Continue in this way until all the cells are complete.

> **Tip**
>
> Don't worry if you get a negative number.

> **Tip**
>
> A formula can use lots of cells, just make sure there is a symbol between each one, for example G1+H1+F1.

Skill 5

Using a function (SUM)

Spreadsheets have **functions** that let you make **specific** calculations without having to type in the symbols, or without having to type the cell references for lots of cells.

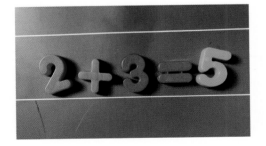

> **Key words**
>
> **Function:** a set of instructions that are followed when a key word is entered.
>
> **Specific:** something particular.

Key word

SUM: a function in a spreadsheet that adds together several numbers.

Tip

Instead of writing the cell references, you can hold your left mouse button down to highlight all the cells you want to use.

Tip

The cells must all be next to each other. You could not use this formula if the cells are A1, B3, B4, C5, and so on, because they are not next to each other.

SUM allows you to add together a range of cells that are next to each other.

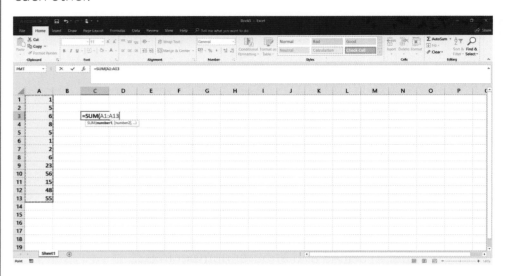

If you want to add together all the numbers in this spreadsheet, the formula would be:

A1+A2+A3+A4+A5+A6+A7+A8+A9+A10+A11+A12+A13

This is a long way of doing it! Instead, you can use SUM to add together lots of numbers.

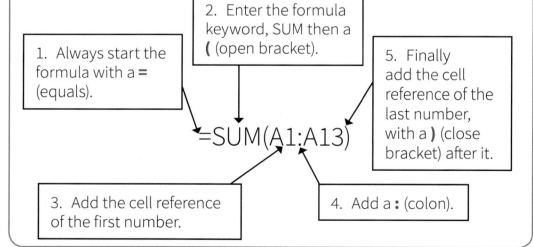

2. Enter the formula keyword, SUM then a **(** (open bracket).

1. Always start the formula with a **=** (equals).

5. Finally add the cell reference of the last number, with a **)** (close bracket) after it.

=SUM(A1:A13)

3. Add the cell reference of the first number.

4. Add a **:** (colon).

Activity 5.1

Open the spreadsheet 'usingSUM.xlsx' that your teacher will give you.

In the cell B9 enter the formula =SUM(B1:B8) to add up all the numbers in cells B1 to B8.

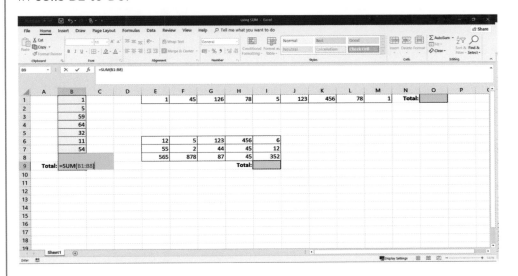

Activity 5.2

Enter a formula in cell O1 to add the cells E1 to M1.

Use the SUM formula.

Activity 5.3

Enter a formula in cell I9 to add the cells E6 to I8.

Use the SUM formula.

Tip

The first cell reference is E1, the last cell reference is M1.

Tip

These cells are all still next to each other, they are just in a rectangle. The first cell reference is E6, the last is I8.

You can click on the **AutoSum** button instead of typing the formula.

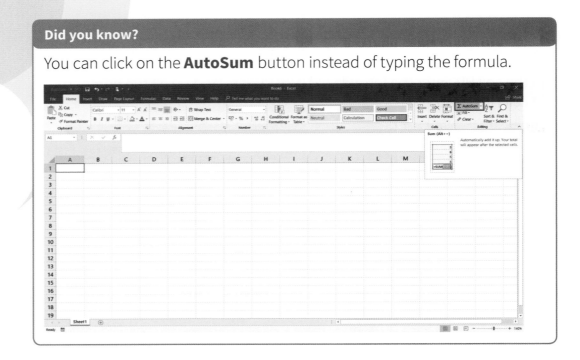

Key words

Replicate: to make a copy of something, for example, a formula.

Data: a single number or word that has no meaning on its own, for example 10.

Skill 6

Copying (or replicating) a formula

You can copy **data** from one place to another, and you can also copy formulas.

When you copy a formula, it changes the cell references that it uses.

There are two ways you can copy a formula.

Method 1

In this example 'Total' has =A2+B2 in it.

You can click on the cell with the formula in (C2) and then click on the **Copy** button in the toolbar.

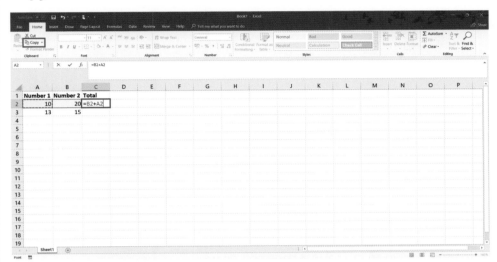

Click on the cell you want the formula copied to (C3) and click on the **Paste** button in the toolbar.

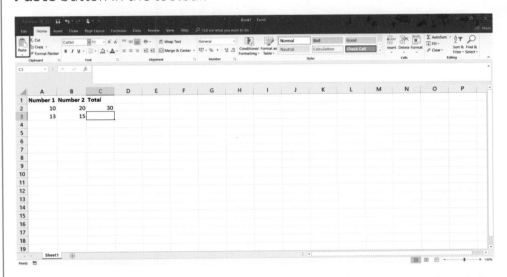

The cell changes the cell references in the formula you pasted, so it is now =A3+B3.

Method 2

When you click on a cell, there is a small square in the bottom right corner of the cell.

This is the Fill Handle.

You can click on the cell with the formula in (C2).

> **Tip**
>
> You can only use the fill handle when the cells are next to each other.

You can then left-click with your mouse on the Fill Handle.

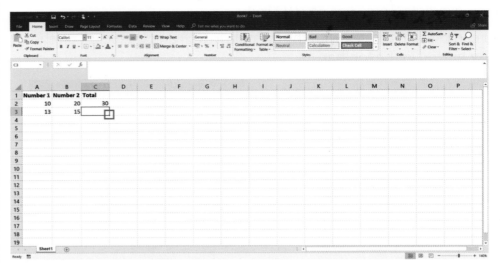

You can hold your left mouse button down and move the cursor to the cell where you want it to appear.

The box will move to surround that cell as well.

If you let go of the mouse button, the formula will be copied.

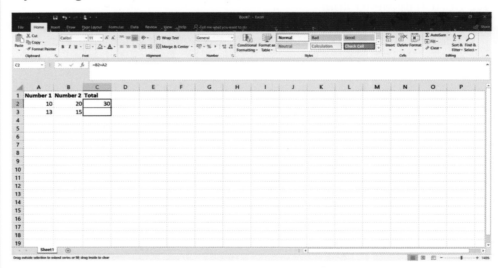

The Fill Handle is useful when you need to copy a formula lots of times.

For these tasks you will need to open the spreadsheet 'copyingformula.xlsx' that your teacher will give you.

Activity 6.1

The formula in cell C2 adds cells A2 and B2.

Copy this formula, using the **Copy** and **Paste** buttons, into cell C3.

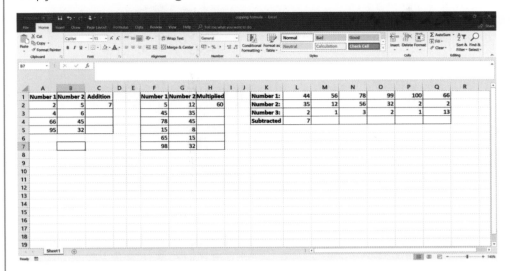

Activity 6.2

Copy the formula you have put in C3, into cells C4 and C5.

Use the Fill Handle.

Activity 6.3

The formula in cell H2 multiplies cell F2 and G2.

Copy this formula, using the **Copy** and **Paste** buttons into cell H3.

Activity 6.4

Copy the formula you have put in H3, into cells H4, H5, H6 and H7.

Use the Fill Handle.

Activity 6.5

The formula in cell L4 is L1–L2–L3.

Copy this formula into cells M4, N4, O4, P4 and Q4.

Use the Fill Handle.

Skill 7

Creating a graph

You can use a spreadsheet to create a graph, for example a bar chart or a pie chart.

You can select the cells you want to use to create a graph, including the titles.

By clicking on the **Insert** tab, you can then choose the type of graph you want.

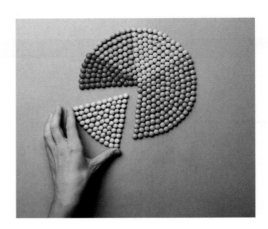

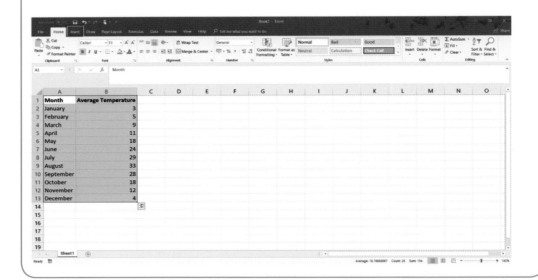

	Month	Average Temperature
1	Month	Average Temperature
2	January	3
3	February	5
4	March	9
5	April	11
6	May	18
7	June	24
8	July	29
9	August	33
10	September	28
11	October	18
12	November	12
13	December	4

You will see a drop-down menu to choose the exact type. Here, you will see a bar chart has been created. (A bar chart is called a column chart in Microsoft Excel.)

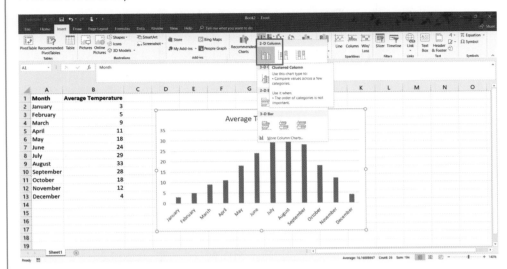

You can change the title by clicking on it and deleting the text.

You can add axis labels by clicking on the graph, then the **+** sign on the top right.

Tick 'Axis titles'.

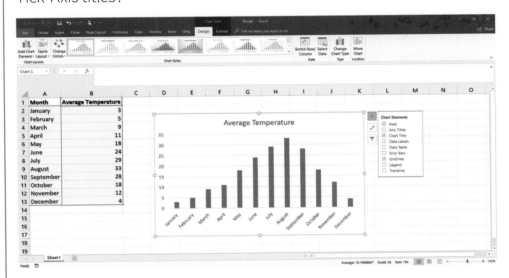

Tip

Remember the *x*-axis is the horizontal, and the *y*-axis is the vertical.

You can also format the text and colours in the graph by right-clicking on any element and changing the options that appear.

To select two columns that are not next to each other, select one, hold down the Ctrl key on the keyboard and select the second.

Activity 7.1

Enter the following data into a spreadsheet.

Day	Temperature
Monday	21
Tuesday	22.5
Wednesday	20
Thursday	23
Friday	19
Saturday	19.5
Sunday	21

Create a bar chart to represent the data.

Make sure your graph has:

- a suitable title
- axis labels.

Tip

Remember that Microsoft Excel calls this a column chart.

Activity 7.2

Create a new spreadsheet. Save it with a meaningful name.

Enter the headings 'Favourite colour' and 'Number of people' into the spreadsheet.

Enter four colours in the 'Favourite colour' column (one on each row).

Ask the people in your class which of the four colours is their favourite.

Enter the results in the 'Number of people' column.

Create a pie chart to show the results.

Skill 8

Modifying data and answering 'what if' questions

You can use spreadsheets to **model** scenarios.

You can look at what might happen, if something changes, without it actually changing in real life. For example:

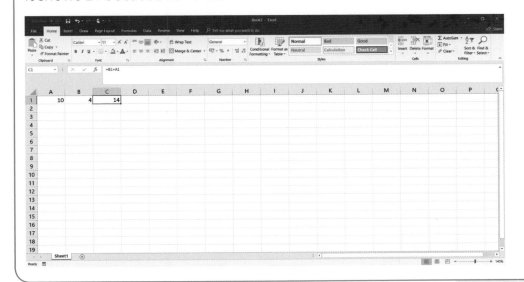

- A shop owner can find out what would happen if they increased the price of one of their products.

- You could use a spreadsheet to work out how much pocket money you would get in a year if it increased by $1 a week.

Spreadsheets can do this because the formulas use cell references to do the calculations, instead of numbers. If you change the numbers used in the calculation, the formula will not change, but it will display the result using the new numbers.

Cell C1 has the formula =A1+B1.

It shows 14 because 10+4=14.

Key words

'What if': a question you can ask, and answer, by changing data values in a spreadsheet to see what they affect and how they change the spreadsheet.

Model: a way of changing items of data to see what happens. You can use a spreadsheet to do this.

The number in cell B1 is changed to 6, and the formula updates the result to 16. 10+6=16.

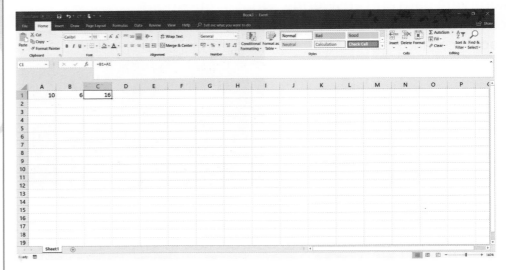

Here you could ask a 'what if' question: 'What will happen if I change the value in cell B1?'

Part of a spreadsheet is shown.

	A	B	C	D
1	10	20	30	
2				
3				

C1 has the formula =A1+B1.

1. What happens if you change A1 to 20?

The value in C1 will change to 40.

2. What happens if you change B1 to 10?

The value in C1 will change to 20.

Activity 8.1

Open the spreadsheet 'manipulatingdata.xlsx' that your teacher will give you.

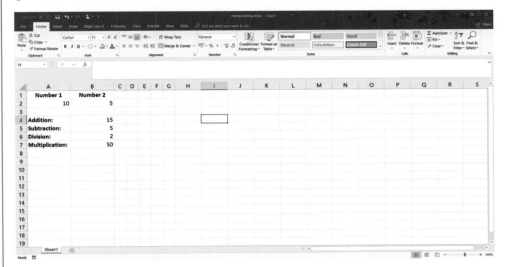

The table shows these formulas.

Cell	Formula
B4	=A2+B2
B5	=A2-B2
B6	=A2/B2
B7	=A2*B2

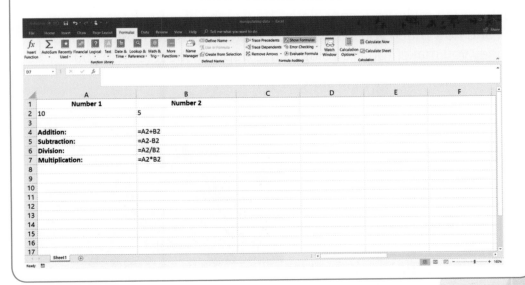

Tip

To see all the formulae in your spreadsheet, click on the **Formula** tab, then 'Show Formulas'. Click on the same button to return to view the data.

Change the number in cell A2 to 20. What changes happen in cells B4 to B7?

_____

_____

Activity 8.2

What will happen if you change the value in B2 from 5 to 10?

_____

Change the value and see if you were correct.

Activity 8.3

In cell H2 enter a formula to add 1 to the value in H1 (=H1+1).

Use the Fill handle to copy this formula along to cell R1.

What will happen if you change the value in H1 to 50?

_____

Change the value and see if you were correct.

Scenario

Chocolate shop

Imagine you own a chocolate shop. You want to work out how much it costs you to make your chocolates, how many of your chocolates you sell and how much you sell them for. You will then work out how much money you make! You are going to use a spreadsheet to help you.

Your spreadsheet needs to store data on:

- the chocolates you sell
- how much each chocolate costs for you to buy
- the price you sell each chocolate for
- how many of each chocolate you have sold
- the total **costs**, **income** and **profit**.

Activity 1

Open the spreadsheet 'chocolateshop.xlsx' that your teacher will give you.

It already has some labels and data in it. Add these labels in the cells listed.

Cell	Label
A9	Total costs
A10	Total income
A11	Profit

Your spreadsheet should look like this image.

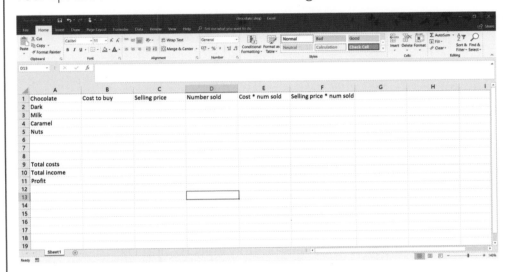

Tip

To change the width of the columns, drag the line between the column letters.

Activity 2

You sell four different types of chocolate at your shop. The table here shows:

- the names of each chocolate
- how much you paid for each chocolate (Cost to buy)
- how much you sell each chocolate for (Selling price).

Enter the cost to buy and selling price into columns B and C.

Chocolate	Cost to buy	Selling price
Dark	1.2	3
Milk	1	2.5
Caramel	0.5	2
Nuts	1	3

Your spreadsheet should look like this:

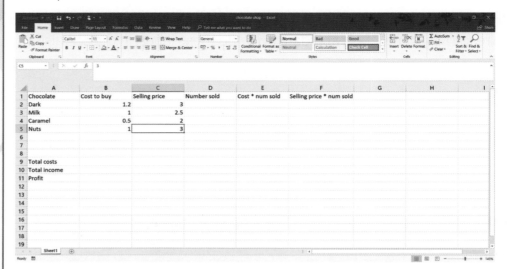

Activity 3

Enter the number 10 in cells D2, D3, D4 and D5 ('Number sold').

Activity 4

Now work out how much it costs to make the chocolate.

The 'Cost * Number sold' column will do:

> 'Cost to buy' (column B) * 'Number sold' (column D)

Enter a formula in cell E2 that will multiply cells B2 and D2.

Copy the formula into cells E3, E4 and E5.

Tip

Use the cell references and the *.

Activity 5

Work out how much income you got from the chocolate.

The 'Selling price * num sold' column will do:

> 'Selling price' (column C) * 'Number sold' (column D)

Enter a formula in cell F2 that will multiply cells C2 and D2.

Copy the formula into cells F3, F4 and F5.

Tip

Use the cell references and the *.

Activity 6

Work out the total cost of buying all the chocolates you have sold.

Enter a formula in cell B9 that will add together all the values in column E (E2, E3, E4 and E5).

Activity 7

Work out the total income your shop has received.

Enter a formula in cell B10 that will add together all the values in column F (F2, F3, F4 and F5).

Activity 8

Work out how much profit your shop has made. This is:

'Total Income' (B10) – 'Total Costs' (B9)

Enter a formula in cell B11 that will subtract the 'Total Costs' (B9) from the 'Total Income' (B10).

Your spreadsheet should now look like this:

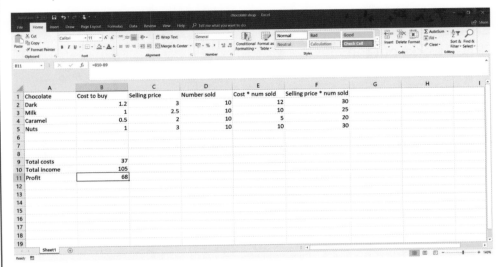

Activity 9

Create a bar chart to show the cost to the shop to buy the chocolates (you will need columns A and B).

Activity 10

What will happen if the number of dark chocolates sold is increased to 20?

_____

_____

Change the data and see if you were correct.

Activity 11

What will happen if the cost to buy Milk chocolates is increased to 2?

_____

_____

Change the data and see if you were correct.

Challenge 1

SUM is only one function that you can use.

There are many others, such as AVERAGE, MIN and MAX.

AVERAGE

AVERAGE works out the average (mean) value from a list. It is used to find a central or typical value of a set of numbers.

The average is calculated by adding up all the values, then dividing by the number of values. by the number of values. For example:

10
2
7
30
6

Add the values together: 10+2+7+30+6=55.

Then divide by the number of values (there are 5 numbers). 55/5=11.

The formula is =AVERAGE(First cell reference:Last cell reference).

For example, =AVERAGE(A1:A3) will work out the average of the values in cells A1, A2 and A3.

MAX

MAX works out the maximum (or largest) value from a list. For example:

| 10 |
| 2 |
| 7 |
| 30 |
| 6 |

The MAX value in this list is 30.

The formula is =MAX(First cell reference:Last cell reference).

For example, =MAX(A1:A3) will work out the largest of the values in cells A1, A2 and A3.

MIN

MIN works out the minimum (or smallest) value from a list. For example:

| 10 |
| 2 |
| 7 |
| 30 |
| 6 |

The MIN value in this list is 2.

The formula is =MIN(First cell reference:Last cell reference).

For example, =MIN(A1:A3) will work out the smallest of the values in cells A1, A2 and A3.

Activity 1

Enter the numbers in the table into cells A1 to A5.

In cell B1, enter the label 'Average'

In cell C1, enter the formula: =AVERAGE(A1:A5).

Activity 2

In cell B2, enter the label 'Max'

In cell C2, enter the formula: =MAX(A1:A5).

Activity 3

In cell B3, enter the label 'Min'

In cell C3, enter the formula: =MIN(A1:A5).

Challenge 2

You can change the way a spreadsheet looks by changing the font style, size and colour of the cells.

It is important to only use these in a few places. Don't start making every cell a different colour as it will make your spreadsheet too complicated.

Open your chocolate shop spreadsheet.

Activity 1

Click on cell A1. Make this cell Bold by clicking on the **B** button on the toolbar.

Centre the cell by clicking on the **Centre** button on the toolbar.

You can also change the font size, style and colour on this toolbar.

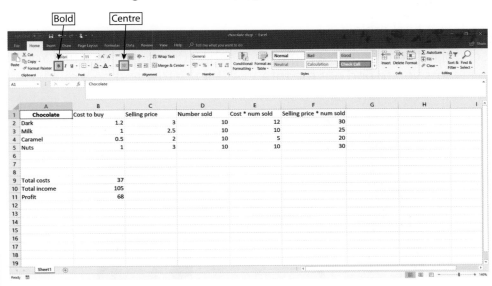

Repeat this for cells A1 to F1.

Make cells A9 to A11 bold.

Activity 2

Highlight the cells A1 to F5.

Click on the **Fill Color** button on the toolbar and chose a light grey.

Click on the arrow on the right of the **Borders** button on the toolbar and choose 'All Borders'.

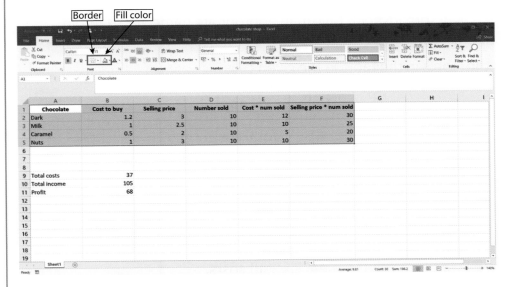

Repeat this with cells A9 to B11.

Final project – School trip time!

Using all the knowledge you have learnt from the skills in this module, you can start your final project.

Your school is taking you on a trip to the Techno Computer Museum. Your teacher wants you to find out the total cost for the trip, and how much each student will need to pay, using a spreadsheet.

The trip will use a coach that costs $500.

Entry to the museum is $5 per student and the guided tour is another $1 per student.

Lunch will cost $2 per student.

The extra staff needed on the trip will cost $200.

Activity 1

Create a new spreadsheet. Give it an appropriate name, for example School trip.

Enter the labels in the table in the given cells.

Cell	Label
A1	Total costs
A2	Item
B2	Cost
A3	Coach
A4	Staff costs

In B3 enter the cost of the coach.

In B4 enter the cost for the extra staff.

Activity 2

Enter the labels in the table in the given cells.

Cell	Label
D1	Cost per student
D2	Item
E2	Cost
D3	Museum entry
D4	Guided tour
D5	Lunch
D6	Coach
D7	Staff

In E3 enter the museum entry cost per student.

In E4 enter the guided tour cost per student.

In E5 enter the lunch cost per student.

Activity 3

The cost of the coach and staff is split evenly between all the students. Each value is divided by the number of students.

In cell G1 enter the label 'Number of students'.

In cell H1 enter the number 20.

This represents the 20 students.

In cell E6 enter a formula that will divide the cost of the coach (B3) by the Number of students (H1).

In cell E7 enter a formula that will divide the staff costs (B4) by the Number of students (H1).

Activity 4

In A9 enter the label 'Total cost per student'.

In B9 enter a formula that will add together all of the costs per student (E3, E4, E5, E6 and E7).

Tip

The divide symbol is /.

Tip

These cells are next to each other, so you can use SUM.

Your spreadsheet should look like this image now.

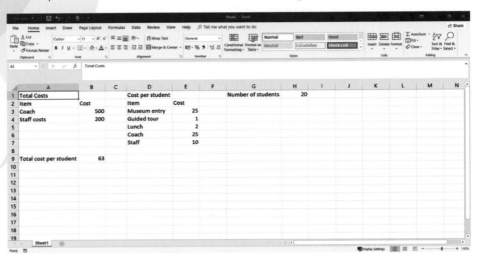

Activity 5

What will happen if you change the cost of the coach to $1000?

_____

_____

What will happen if you change the number of students to 40?

_____

_____

What will happen if you change the museum entry cost per student to $10?

_____

_____

What will happen if you change the staff costs to $10?

_____

_____

Activity 6

Create a pie chart to show the cost per student of all five items.

You will need to highlight cells D2 to E7.

Make sure you add an appropriate graph title.

Activity 7

Make the labels in your spreadsheet bold and centred.

Change the cell colour and border of cells with data in.

Activity 8

Print out a copy of your spreadsheet showing the data, and a copy of your spreadsheet showing the formulas.

Reflection

1 Why are spreadsheet models useful?

_____

_____

_____

_____

_____

_____

2 Why is it better to use a spreadsheet for calculations, instead of doing it on paper?

_____

_____

_____

_____

_____

	In this module, you will learn how to:	Pass/Merit	Done?
1	Add new records to a data file	P	
2	Identify field types	P	
3	Use 'equals', 'more than' and 'less than' in searches	P	
4	Re-write a question using search criteria	M	
5	Interpret data.	M	

In this module you are going to develop skills to help you work towards your final project, which is about imaginary creatures that have just been discovered living on a deserted island! In the project you will be using a database about these imaginary creatures. You will add new imaginary creatures and use search criteria to find out information about the creatures.

You will also learn how to:

- use 'NOT' in a search
- use 'more than and equal to' and 'less than and equal to' in a search.

Before you start

You should:

- know how to search using keywords
- be familiar with finding **information**, for example by searching the internet using a search engine
- have experience of working with **data**, for example collecting data, and reading and interpreting data (making sense of what data means). You might have done this when you have created graphs and tables.

Introduction

All organisations, companies, and so on, store data. They might store data about the people who work for them, about the items they sell and about how much money they make. This data can be stored in lots of different ways, for example, using a spreadsheet, a **database** or just entering data into a word-processed document. In this module you will learn about how data is stored in a database, and how you can search that database to find information.

Key words

Information: this is data that has meaning; you can understand what it is telling you, for example, 12 horses.

Data: numbers or words that have no meaning on their own, for example, 25 or database.

Database: a collection of data held in tables.

Skill 1

What is a database?

A database is a system that stores data in a structured, organised way. It is a data **file**, which means it stores data in a document.

Activity 1.1

Imagine you have lots of information that you need to organise about four patients in a hospital, for example:

Jen is a patient in ward 2a. She has the patient ID (identification) 12AB5 and was born on the 1st February 1975. Jen's second name is Cardi.

Odo Tembe is another patient, but he is in ward 5b. Odo was born on 16/3/1968 and has the ID number 55KKL.

A third patient, Nishith Patel, is in the same ward as Jen. Miss Patel has the patient ID 77EJ9 and was born in 1983 (8th December).

The final patient is on ward 3a. This patient has the ID 19HH1. He was born on 02/02/1982 and is named Muhammed Malouf.

Write down the patient IDs of all patients in ward 2a.

_____

_____

The information here is muddled and difficult to read easily. It is easier to find specific pieces of information if they are organised into a table:

Patient ID	First name	Second name	Date of birth	Ward number
12ABS	Jen	Cardi	01/02/1975	2a
55KKI	Odo	Tembe	16/03/1968	5b
19HH1	Muhammed	Malouf	02/02/1982	3a
77EJ9	Nishith	Patel	08/12/1983	2a

Write down the second name of all patients in ward 2a.

_____

_____

Searching a table for specific information is easier and quicker because the data is organised, for example, in a database.

Key word

File: a document, for example a database, that is stored in a computer.

Activity 1.2

A database is made up of one or more tables. Each table stores data about one topic; for example, a hospital has a table about patients, a table about doctors, a table about appointments, and so on.

Each table is made up of lots of pieces of information that are organised in **fields**. For example, a table about patients might store their first name, second name, date of birth and so on. Each of these are fields.

When a table is filled in with data, each **row** of data is about one item, object or person. In a table about patients, each row is about one patient. This is called a **record**.

Databases come in many forms, and there are many different pieces of software you can use. Microsoft Access is one example of database software. You will be using Microsoft Access throughout this module to add data to databases and to search for specific information.

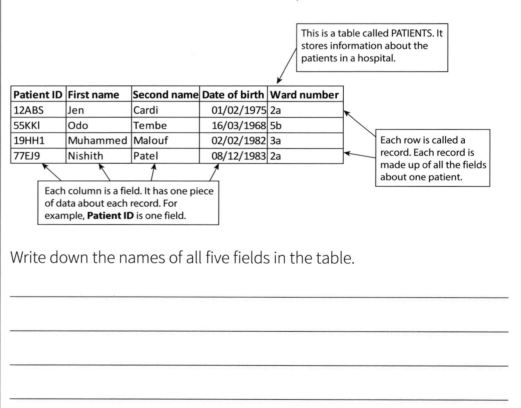

This is a table called PATIENTS. It stores information about the patients in a hospital.

Patient ID	First name	Second name	Date of birth	Ward number
12ABS	Jen	Cardi	01/02/1975	2a
55KKI	Odo	Tembe	16/03/1968	5b
19HH1	Muhammed	Malouf	02/02/1982	3a
77EJ9	Nishith	Patel	08/12/1983	2a

Each row is called a record. Each record is made up of all the fields about one patient.

Each column is a field. It has one piece of data about each record. For example, **Patient ID** is one field.

Write down the names of all five fields in the table.

_____

_____

_____

_____

_____

Write down the Patient IDs of all four records in the table.

_____

_____

_____

_____

Skill 2

Identifying fields

Activity 2.1

Think about your school. It will store data about you: one piece of data will be your first name. This field will be called first name.

Write three other fields that the school might store about you.

_____

_____

_____

Activity 2.2

Compare your list with a friend's list.

Do you have similar answers? Add any new fields to your list.

Activity 2.3

Superheroes all have a superhero name. They also have a real first name and second name.

Superheroes have a gender, for example, male or female.

Some superheroes can fly.

Some superheroes can become invisible.

Some superheroes wear masks.

Each superhero has a date of birth and a height (in cm).

Each superhero has a main colour for their clothes, and a country where they live.

Some superheroes also have another special ability.

A database is needed to store all this data about superheroes.

Write a list of fields that could be used to store the data described for the superheroes.

_____

_____

_____

_____

Skill 3

Data types

Computers need to know what type of data you want them to store. For example, will the field need to store a number? Will it need to store letters?

The table describes some common data types you find in a database.

Data type	Description	Examples
Text	This will store letters (a-z, A-Z), symbols (for example, !,./") and numbers that you will not do calculations with (for example, a telephone number).	• Hello • this is all text!! • This is also text 123 • 0028374637282
Number	This will only store numbers.	• 123 • 5 • 2.6 • 59865212356
Date	This will store dates, that is, day, month, year (you can change the **order** you want it displayed in).	• 1/2/1990 • 12/12/1953
Boolean	This will only store Yes or No.	• Yes • No
Currency	This will store numbers with a currency symbol, for example, £, $.	• £2.00 • $3999.99

Key word

Order: the arrangement of items, for example alphabetical order.

A person's first name uses letters. The only data type that allows letters is Text. The data type for the field 'First Name' is Text.

A person's age uses numbers. You might want to do calculations with the number, for example, add ten to it. The data type for the field 'Age' is 'Number'.

A question with only two possible answers can be stored as a Boolean, for example: Do you have a television? Yes or No.

Activity 3.1

Write all the fields you identified for the superheroes, followed by the most appropriate data type to store that data.

_____

_____

_____

_____

Activity 3.2

Compare your answers to a friend's. Are they similar? If not, explain why you chose the data type you chose. Get your friend to explain the data type they chose. Decide which is the most appropriate.

Skill 4

Navigating a database

Your teacher will supply you with a superhero database. You need to open the database, then the table to view the superheroes.

Activity 4.1

Open the database file named 'superheroes.accdb'.

Double-click on 'Superheroes' as shown:

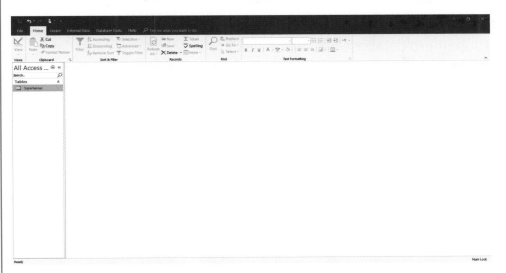

The table will open and show you the data about the superheroes that are already in the database.

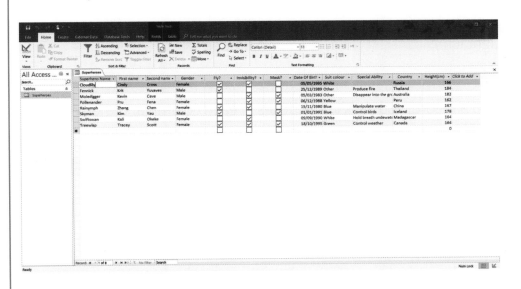

Activity 4.2

Look at the fields you identified in **Skill 2 Activity 2.3**. Compare these to the ones in the table and identify any you missed out.

Add a new record

The superhero database has twelve fields. The field names and data types are:

Field name	Data type
Superhero Name	Text
First name	Text
Second name	Text
Gender	Text
Fly?	Boolean
Invisibility?	Boolean
Mask?	Boolean
Date of Birth	Date
Suit Colour	Text
Special Ability	Text
Country	Text
Height (cm)	Number

As you have already learnt, a record is a row of data.

To add a record, you click in the boxes in each column and then enter your data.

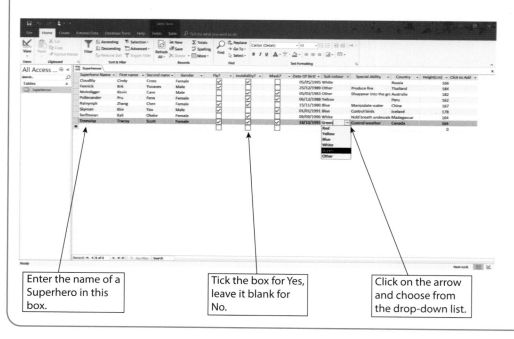

Enter the name of a Superhero in this box.

Tick the box for Yes, leave it blank for No.

Click on the arrow and choose from the drop-down list.

Activity 5.1

Add two new superheroes to your database.

You can leave a field empty if it is not appropriate for your superheroes.

You cannot leave 'Superhero Name' empty.

Activity 5.2

Ask your friends about their superheroes.

Add their superheroes to your database.

Make sure you have at least five new superheroes in your database.

Skill 6

Writing a query with the EQUALS criteria

You can search a database for specific information that you want to find. You do this using a **query**.

You can enter search **criteria** to narrow down what you want to find. For example, if you want to find all people who are Female, then Gender as female is your criteria.

Key words

Query: a database tool that lets you search for specific data, returning a subset of the data.

Criteria: the requirements you specify you are looking for, for example, Age = 20.

Subset: a small part of the whole. That is, the results of a query will return some data, but not all of it.

The query returns a **subset** of the data (a new table that just shows what you are looking for).

Activity 6.1

Search for the superhero names of all the female superheroes.

To create a query, make sure your database table is closed (click on the cross on the top right-hand corner of the table).

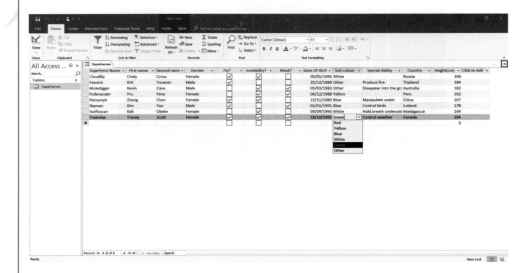

Click on **Create**.

Click on the **Query Design** button.

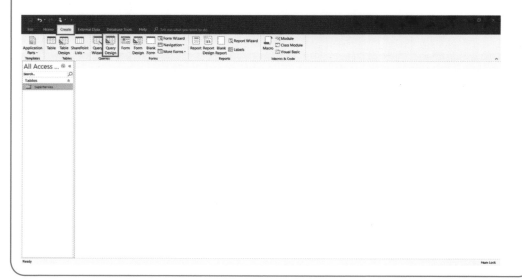

Click on the Superhero table name, then click on 'Add'.

Click on 'Close'.

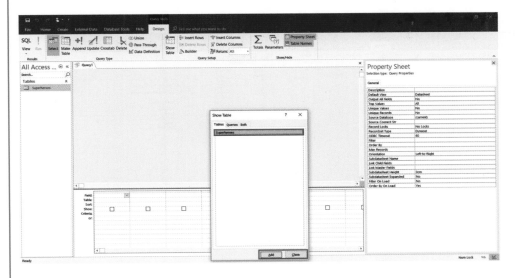

Double-click on all the fields you want to display in your query. You want the superhero names of all female superheroes so you need the fields 'Superhero Name' and 'Gender'.

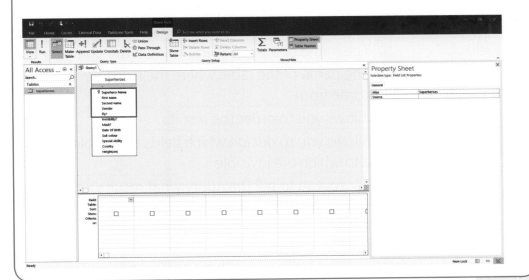

The fields you have double-clicked appear below.

In the image there is an extra field: 'First name'. To delete it, just delete the text 'First name' where it is highlighted in the red box.

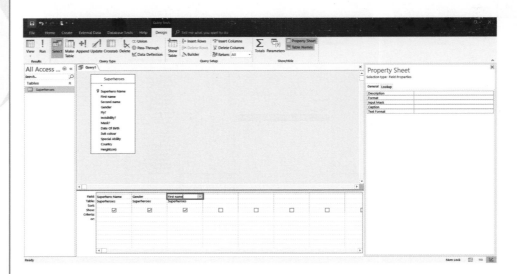

Now you need to enter your criteria.

The rows in the table are:

Row name	Description
Field	The name of the fields you want in the query
Table	The name of the table where the fields have come from
Sort	Allows you to order the results
Show	Allows you to decide which fields are visible and which are invisible
Criteria	Allows you to tell the query what results you want
Or	Allows you to enter another criteria

The criteria you are using is for superheroes who are female. You want the gender to be female.

Find the 'Gender' field in the table, and in the 'Criteria' box below it, enter 'Female'. You don't need to enter speech marks; Microsoft Access will do this for you.

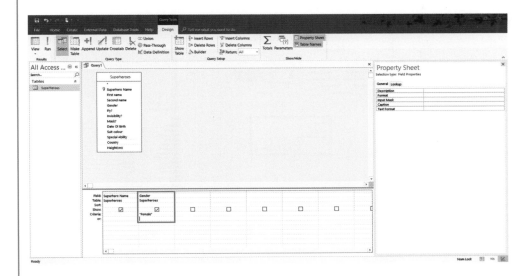

To save your query click on **File** and **Save**.

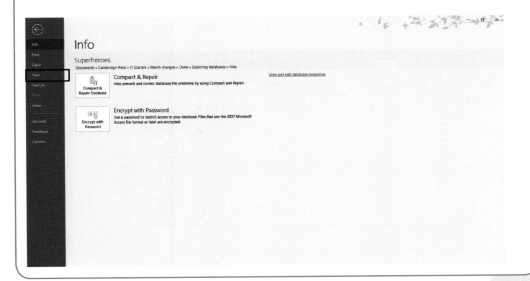

Microsoft Access will ask you to give your query a name.

Give it an appropriate name that describes the query, for example 'Female superheroes'.

Click on 'OK'.

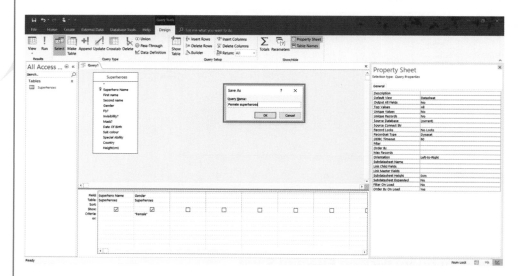

Click on **Run** at the top of the screen to see the results.

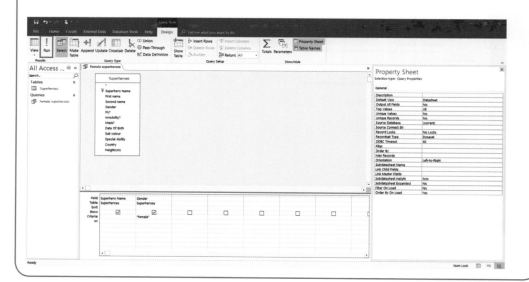

A new table will appear with the fields you selected. Only female superheroes should be displayed.

If it hasn't worked, then you might need to check your spellings.

Click on the **View** button, then 'Design View' to change your query.

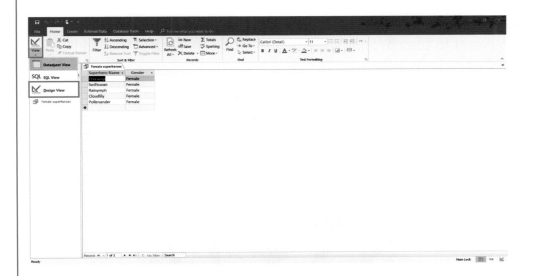

To close your query, click on the cross on the right-hand side.

Your query name will appear on the left. You can open it again by double-clicking on it.

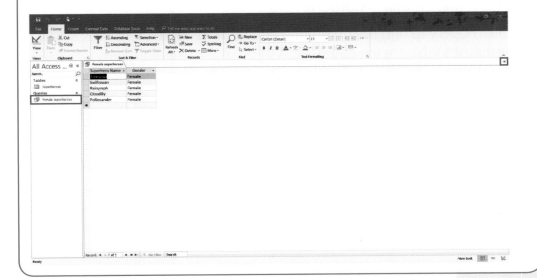

Activity 6.2

Create a query to find all male superheroes.

You will need the fields 'Superhero Name' and 'Gender'.

The criteria for gender is 'Male'.

Activity 6.3

If you want to search for all superheroes who can fly, then the field 'Fly?' would need to be ticked.

The criteria for 'Fly?' is 'Yes'.

Create a query to find the suit colour of all superheroes who can fly.

Activity 6.4

You can enter criteria in **numeric** fields.

Create a query to find the first name and second name of all superheroes who are exactly 164 cm tall.

The 164 will not have speech marks around it, because it is a number.

Activity 6.5

You can enter criteria in date fields.

Enter the date you are searching for in the criteria. Microsoft Access will put # around the date for you, for example '#5/5/2017#'.

Create a query to find the superhero name, and Height(cm) of superheroes born on 05/03/1983.

Activity 6.6

Create your own query to find out information about the superheroes in your database.

Identify which fields you want to see, and what criteria you want to enter.

Skill 7

Using < and > in searches

Queries on fields that have the data type number can use < and > in the criteria.

These work the same way as they work in mathematics.

< means less than.

> means greater than.

Activity 7.1

10 < 20 is True because 10 is less than 20.

15 < 10 is False because 15 is not less than 20.

3 < 3 is False because 3 is not less than 3, it is the same as 3.

a Is 9 < 10?

_____

b Is 100 < 200?

_____

c Is 29 < 22?

_____

d Is 55 < 55?

_____

Activity 7.2

40 > 30 is True because 40 is greater than 30.

101 > 100 is True because 101 is greater than 100.

5 > 5 is False because 5 is not greater than 5, it is the same as 5.

a Is 66 > 3?

_____

b Is 999 > 3?

_____

c Is 13 > 15?

_____

d Is 999 > 999?

_____

Activity 7.3

We can use < and > in queries as the criteria to find all records that are less than, or greater than, the number entered.

For example, to find all superheroes who are less than 170 cm in height, the criteria would be '< 170'.

To find all superheroes who are more than 170 cm in height, the criteria would be '> 170'.

Create a query to find the superhero name of all superheroes who are less than 170 cm in height.

Create the query in the same way you would for an EQUALS query. Add the fields 'Superhero Name' and 'Height(cm)'.

In the Criteria box for 'Height(cm)' enter <170. There are no speech marks because it is a number field.

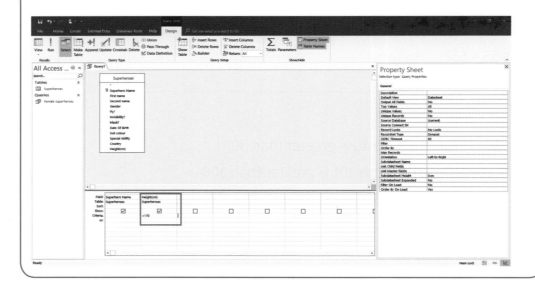

Activity 7.4

Create a query to find the First name and Second name of all superheroes who are more than 172 cm tall.

Activity 7.5

You can also use < and > with dates.

Create a query to find the Second name, and whether the superhero can fly, for all superheroes born before 1990. This means they must have been born before 01/01/1990.

Add the fields 'Second name', 'Fly?' and 'Date Of Birth'.

Add the criteria '<01/01/1990' under 'Date Of Birth'.

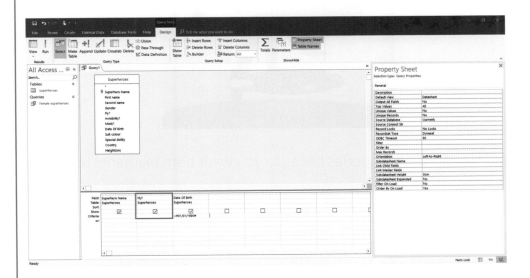

Activity 7.6

Create a query to find the Special Ability of all superheroes who are more than 175 cm tall.

Activity 7.7

Create a query to find the Superhero Name and Suit colour of superheroes who are less than 165 cm tall.

AND queries

You can create a query that has more than one criteria. For example finding the superhero names of all superheroes who can fly and who wear a mask.

These are called AND queries because you want both elements to be true.

Activity 8.1

Clap your hands if you are male and your favourite colour is green.

a If you are male and your favourite colour was blue, would you clap your hands?

_____

b If you are female and your favourite colour is green, would you clap your hands?

_____

c If you are male and your favourite colour is green, would you clap your hands?

_____

Activity 8.2

Create a query with the fields 'Superhero Name', 'Fly?' and 'Mask?'.

In the criteria row, enter 'Yes' under the field 'Fly?'. Also write 'Yes' under the field 'Mask?'. Both criteria must be on the same row.

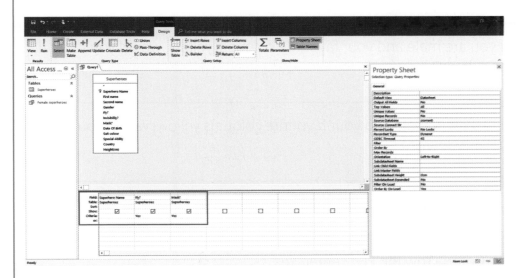

Activity 8.3

Create a query to find the countries of superheroes who are male <u>and</u> can fly.

Activity 8.4

Create a query to find the suit colours of all superheroes who can become invisible <u>and</u> can fly.

Tip

The fields you need are 'Country', 'Fly?' and 'Gender'. The criteria for 'Fly?' will be 'Yes'. The criteria for 'Gender' will be 'Male'.

Tip

The fields you need are 'Suit Colour', 'Invisibility?' and 'Fly?'. The criteria for 'Invisibility' and 'Fly?' are both 'Yes'.

Skill 9

OR queries

A statement with OR in it means one or both options. For example, you may want to find all superheroes who can fly, or who wear a mask.

An OR query would show all the superheroes who can fly, and it would also show all the superheroes who wear a mask.

Key word

OR: a database command. It searches for data that matches one, or both sides of the OR statement.

Activity 9.1

Jump up and down if you are female or your favourite colour is yellow.

a If you are female and your favourite colour is red, would you jump up and down?

_____

b If you are male and your favourite colour is yellow, would you jump up and down?

_____

c If you are female and your favourite colour is yellow, would you jump up and down?

_____

Activity 9.2

Create a query to find all superheroes who can fly, or who wear a mask.

In the Criteria row for 'Fly?', enter 'Yes'.

In the row beneath 'Criteria', with the title 'or:', enter 'Yes' for the field 'Mask?'.

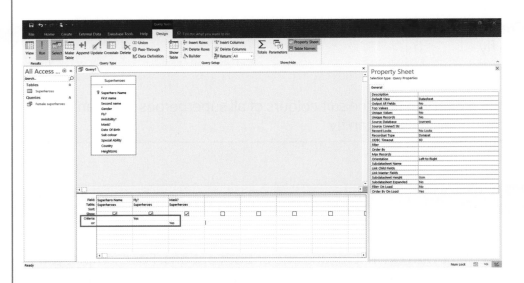

You can put as many ORs as you want, just make sure each one goes on a new line.

Activity 9.3

Create a query to find the first name and second name of superheroes who are male <u>or</u> who can become invisible.

> **Tip**
>
> The fields needed are 'First name', 'Second name', 'Gender' and 'Invisibility?'. You will need 'Male' for the 'Gender' criteria, and 'Yes' for the 'Invisibility?' criteria. Make sure these are on separate lines.

Activity 9.4

Create a query to find the suit colour of superheroes who can either turn invisible <u>or</u> fly.

Activity 9.5

Create a query to find the date of birth of superheroes who are less than 165 cm tall <u>or</u> are greater than 175 cm tall.

Skill 10

INCLUDES queries

You might not know exactly what you are looking for, but you know that it might include specific letters or words. For example, you want to find superheroes who have 'gg' in their name.

The asterisk symbol, *, means 'anything' in a query. For example:

- '*gg' will find all data that ends in 'gg'. There can be anything before it, but nothing after.
- 'gg*' will find all data that has 'gg' at the start, followed by any data after it.
- '*gg*' will find all data that has 'gg' anywhere in it. There can be anything in front of it and anything after it.

In Microsoft Access, the keyword 'Like' is also required.

To search for superhero names that end in an 'n' you would enter the criteria 'Like *n'.

Tip

You will need the 'Date Of Birth' field and 'Height(cm)'. The 'Height(cm)' field will need <u>two</u> criteria, the first < 165, then underneath >175.

Key word

INCLUDES: a database command to return data items that include the letters and/or numbers that come after it.

Did you know?

An asterisk * in searches is called a wildcard.

Tip

Remember, all text is case sensitive. A capital **N** is not the same as a lowercase **n**.

Activity 10.1

Look at the data in the table.

Icon
Falcon
Zircon
Fairy
Lexicon
Lemonade
Furry
Zebra

Write down the words that will be returned if we used the search: '*con'.

_____

Activity 10.2

Write down the words from the table that will be returned if we used the search: 'Z*'.

_____

Activity 10.3

Write down the words from the table that will be returned if we used the search: '*I*'.

_____

Activity 10.4

Search the superheroes database for the names of all superheroes whose name starts with an 'S', together with their special ability.

Create a new query. Select the fields 'Superhero Name' and 'Special Ability'.

You want the Superhero Name to start with an S, so you don't want anything before it – but anything can come after it.

The search criteria is 'Like S*'.

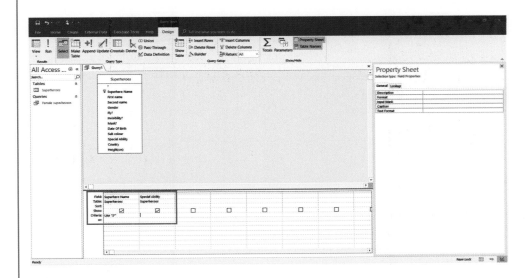

Activity 10.5

Create a query to find the suit colour of all superheroes whose Superhero Name ends in the letter r.

Activity 10.6

Create a query to find the date of birth of all superheroes whose special ability includes the word water.

Activity 10.7

You can use 'Like' on fields with number and date data types.

For example, you can find all superheroes who were born in 1988 by using the criteria 'Like *1988'.

You can find all superheroes who were born in November by using the criteria 'Like */11/*'.

Find the superhero name of all superheroes who were born in 1988.

Select the fields 'Superhero Name' and 'Date Of Birth'. Enter the criteria 'Like *1988' in the criteria for 'Date Of Birth'.

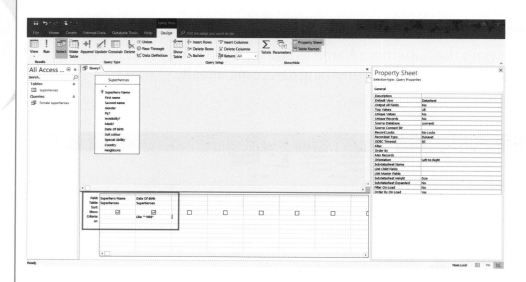

Activity 10.8

Create a query to find the First name and Second name of all superheroes who were born in December.

Skill 11

Sorting

To sort means to put something in an order. For example, you can sort books into alphabetical order, or order by author.

Orders can be ascending or descending.

Ascending means increasing from small to large. The smallest number would appear first. If using letters, the letter 'a' would be first.

Descending means decreasing from large to small. The largest number would appear first. If using letters, the letter 'z' would be first.

Activity 11.1
Put the following numbers into ascending numerical order.

22, 5, 18, 10, 99, 1, 5

Activity 11.2
Put the following numbers into descending numerical order.

22, 5, 18, 10, 99, 1, 5

Activity 11.3
Put the following words into ascending alphabetical order.

lexicon, icon, falcon, zircon, fairy, furry, zebra

Activity 11.4
Put the following words into descending alphabetical order.

lexicon, icon, falcon, zircon, fairy, furry, zebra

Activity 11.5
You can sort query results.

Find the superhero name, gender and date of birth of all superheroes. Display the results in ascending order of date of birth (oldest to youngest).

Select the fields 'Superhero Name', 'Date Of Birth', 'Gender'.

Criteria should be left blank as we want all superheroes.

Click in the row labelled 'Sort', under the field 'Date Of Birth'. You will get the options 'Ascending' and 'Descending'. Choose 'Ascending'.

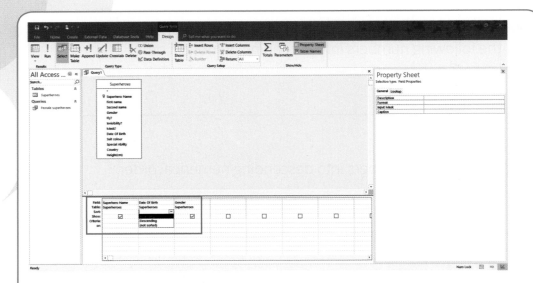

Tip

You don't need any criteria. The sort will be under 'Superhero Name', and will be 'Ascending'.

Activity 11.6

Create a query to display all the superhero names, whether they can fly, and if they can become invisible.

Order the results in ascending order of superhero name.

Activity 11.7

Create a query to display the superhero name of all superheroes who have the suit colour blue.

Order the results in descending order of superhero name.

Activity 11.8

Create a query to display the country and height of all superheroes.

Order the results in descending order of height.

Skill 12

Rephrasing a question as a query and interpreting the results

All of the queries you've been asked to create have been very structured (you've been given the field names and search criteria, and so on). Sometimes, when you need to search for information, you won't be given this structure – you will need to come up with it yourself.

Activity 12.1

Key City is under threat from the evil Doctor Darkly! Only a superhero who can fly can save the day. Who can we ask to help?

You need to rephrase the question as a query.

Step 1: Identify which fields you need. Do you need to know the superhero name? Do you need to know their first name or their second name, and so on? Work through each field and decide which fields you need.

Step 2: Is there any criteria you need to enter? Which field do you need? What is the criteria?

Step 3: Do you need to sort the results in any specific order?

For this query we are going to need:

- Superhero Name
- Fly?

The criteria for Fly? will be Yes. You might have other fields that you think are important – that is ok! If you think they are important, then keep them in.

Create the query.

Once you have run the query you can interpret the findings. Interpreting means looking at the results and deciding what they mean, or what they show. It might mean using the data to answer a question.

Which superheroes can help Key City? Answer the question to interpret the data.

Activity 12.2

Key City is being attacked again. This time by Sandy Sam. The people of Key City need a superhero who can turn invisible, and who is at least 168 cm tall. Who can help them?

Turn the question into a query, then answer the question.

Activity 12.3

A mega-storm is about to strike Key City. They need a superhero who does not fly (otherwise they will get swept away by the wind). The people want to ask the oldest superhero to help first. Which superheroes can help Key City? Which superhero should they ask first?

Turn the question into a query, then answer the question.

Scenario

Favourite books

You have been asked by your teacher to collect data about some books and store them in a database.

Activity 1

Collect a set of ten books. Identify the fields you could use to represent the information about the books.

Activity 2

Open the database file 'myBooks.accdb' that your teacher will give you. Look at the table Books to see the following image.

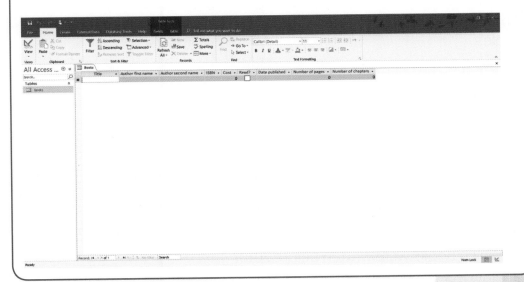

The fields are:

Field	Description	Example data	Data type
Title	The title of the book	Jane Eyre	
Author first name	The first name of the author (if there is more than one, just give one)	Charlotte	
Author second name	The second name of the author (if there is more than one, just give one)	Brontë	
ISBN	The unique number for the book, usually found on the back	978-00079023 61	
Cost	The cost of the book	25.99	
Read?	Whether you have read the book or not	Yes (box is ticked)	
Date published	The date the book was published (if only a year is given then use 1st January as the day and month)	01/01/2005	
Number of pages	The number of pages in the book	200	
Number of chapters	The number of chapters in the book	18	

For each field, write the most appropriate data type for the data in the table.

Activity 3
Open the database table Books and add at least ten books to the table, filling in every field for each book.

Activity 4
Create a query to find the answers to the following questions:

a What are the titles of all the books you have read?

b Which authors have written books with more than 200 pages?

c Which books were written before 2010?

d How many pages are in books with more than 10 chapters?

e What is the title and ISBN number of books that cost more than $10?

f Which books have more than 100 pages and more than 10 chapters?

Activity 5

Create four queries of your own.

a Decide what you would like to find out.

b Decide which fields need to be used.

c Create the queries and enter your criteria.

d Interpret your results.

Challenge

Activity 1

As well as AND and OR searches, there is also an option for **NOT**. For example you want all superheroes except those whose suit colour is red.

The image shows this query:

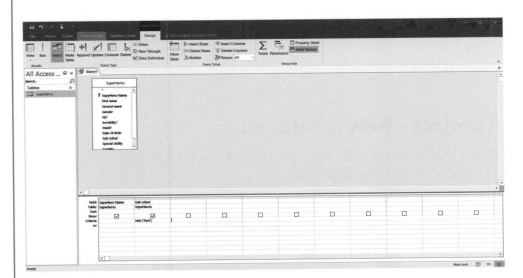

Key word

NOT: a database command. It searches for data that does not match what follows the NOT statement.

The criteria for Suit colour is 'Not("Red")'. The data you put inside the brackets is what will not be selected. If this is text based you need to make sure it is in speech marks ("").

Create a query to display all the superhero names that do not have the suit colour blue.

Create a query to display all the superheroes' first and second names who do not live in a specific country (for example Peru).

Activity 2

In mathematics you not only have < and >, you also have <= and >=. You can use these in criteria too.

>= means greater than or equal to.

<= means less than or equal to.

For example 10 <= 20 is true, because 10 is less than 20.

10 <= 10 is also true, because 10 is equal to 10.

11 <= 10 is false, because 11 is not less than 10 and it is not equal to 10.

19 >= 20 is false, because 19 is not greater than 20 and it is not equal to 20.

20 >= 20 is true, because 20 is equal to 20.

21 >= 20 is true, because 21 is greater than 20.

Create a query to find all superheroes who are less than or equal to 164 cm in height.

Create a query to find all superheroes who were born on or after (>=) 05/05/1995.

Final project – New creatures!

A group of creatures has just been discovered living on a deserted island! Two of these creatures are described below.

The Iggilydog is a land-based animal that has eight legs. It is red and black and only has one eye. The Iggilydog that was found is 110 cm long and 55 cm high, and it weighs 6 kg. The Iggilydog has been seen swimming in the ocean.

The Kimmaeel is a water-based animal. It doesn't have any legs because it lives and swims in the ocean. The Kimmaeel is only 8 cm long and 1.5 cm high; it weighs 0.1 kg. The Kimmaeel is pink and grey.

Activity 1
Identify the fields needed to store the information about the imaginary creatures.

Activity 2
Identify the most appropriate data types for the fields you have identified.

Activity 3
Open the database 'imaginaryCreatures.accdb' that you teacher will give you. Open the table Creatures. Add the information about the Iggilydog and the Kimmaeel to the database.

Activity 4
Add another ten creatures to the database.

Activity 5
Create queries to find answers to the following questions:

a What are the names of all the creatures that have legs?

b Which creatures have legs and can swim?

c How much do the creatures that are more than 50 cm long weigh?

d Which creatures have red as at least one of their colours?

e Which ocean-living creatures also have the colour pink?

f Which creatures are more than 20 cm long, more than 20 cm high, and weigh more than 5 kg?

Activity 6
Create six queries of your own and interpret the results.

Reflection

Think about the following.

1 Why are databases used to store information?

_____

_____

2 A school has a database about its students and their grades. What information would teachers want to find out about their students and grades?

_____

_____

_____

_____

_____

_____

3 Databases can also be paper based. Why would an electronic database be better than a paper-based database?

_____

_____

_____

_____

_____

_____